CLUTTER BUSTING

...etting Go of What's Holding You Back

BROOKS PALMER

Praise for *Clutter Busting*

"Before I even finished this book, I had to start implementing some of the recommendations. By the time I read the last page, not only my home but also my family dynamic and my career were unrecognizable. It was like a miracle."

— Debra Halperin Poneman, founder of
Yes to Success Seminars and bestselling author of
Chicken Soup for the American Idol Soul

"Before reading *Clutter Busting* I was a clutter collector: on my desk, in my basement, and in that dark cave I call my closet. I have needed this book for years, and I loved it! Brooks's advice helped me clean up this clutter, which gave me more time, energy, and creativity. We should start a clutter-busting club — we'd all be better off!"

— Robert J. Kriegel, PhD, *New York Times*
bestselling author of *If It Ain't Broke, Break It!*
and *Sacred Cows Make the Best Burgers*

"Brooks Palmer offers solid advice for those wanting to clear the clutter from their physical and mental spaces. Palmer makes the important connection between internal and external spaces and shows how clearing one area positively affects the other. A great resource."

— Katherine Gibson, author of *Unclutter Your Life:
Transforming Your Physical, Mental, and Emotional Space*

CLUTTER BUSTING

CLUTTER BUSTING

Letting Go of What's Holding You Back

BROOKS PALMER

New World Library
Novato, California

New World Library
14 Pamaron Way
Novato, California 94949

Text design by Tona Pearce Myers

Library of Congress Cataloging-in-Publication Data
Palmer, Brooks.
Clutter busting : letting go of what's holding you back / Brooks Palmer.
   p.   cm.
 ISBN 978-1-57731-659-6 (pbk. : alk. paper)
1. House cleaning. 2. Storage in the home. 3. Orderliness. I. Title.
TX324.P33 2009
648'.5—dc22   2008048887

First printing, March 2009
ISBN 978-1-57731-659-6
Printed in the USA on 100% postconsumer-waste recycled paper

 New World Library is a proud member of the Green Press Initiative.

20 19 18 17 16 15 14 13 12

With all the things you have in your life,
are you any more happy than your dog?

—— RAMESH BALSEKAR

CONTENTS

INTRODUCTION

It's time for you to take out the trash.

Currently you live in the most expensive type of trash can. The trash in your home (or work environment) consumes precious space and zaps energy from your life. It is time to make the place you live your home again. It's time to renew your energy. It's time to take out the trash. What trash, you ask?

Trash, or clutter, includes the things that you hold on to that are no longer useful to you. These things may be worn-out or brand-new, but they are trash because they have lost their value. Such things no longer serve a purpose, and they certainly don't add to your quality of life. They are barriers to good, powerful, and necessary change.

The clothes you no longer wear, the papers choking your desk and files, the electronics you've replaced, the extraneous and unused items stuffed into your kitchen cabinets and drawers, the CDs you no longer listen to: all the various things that clog up your home, office, and garage constantly trip you up in every area of your life. Whether or not you realize it, these "white elephants" are the reason you no longer enjoy your home; they are behind that feeling of "I just can't get anything done" and general feelings of unhappiness, illness, and disease. Collectively, they are overwhelming your senses. Nothing motivates you anymore. You can never get organized. Tasks go unfinished; projects get left behind. You feel buried, unaccomplished. You feel as if you need *something* to feel better.

What *do* you need to feel better? How do you start to make changes? How can you begin to take care of yourself and your surroundings if you haven't done so for months, maybe even years?

This book is about what I call "clutter busting": actively breaking through barriers and letting go of the unnecessary clutter that crowds your life. Clutter busting helps restore clarity and insight. When you clutter bust, you find yourself. You remove the impediments to a happy life. You naturally replace lack of motivation, anxiety, and unhappiness with peace of mind, certainty, and acceptance of change and progress.

It is your clutter. It is your decision. Your things are beneficial only when they improve or enhance your life in some way. This book will help you decide what stays and what *goes*!

The process will be easy if you are open to letting go. If you struggle with letting go, don't worry. I will advise you along the way, providing plenty of examples from real-life clutter bustings. I will give you the necessary tools for you to reclaim your life. You'll find yourself tossing the trash into the trash can, where it belongs. It's time for you to take back your space — and your life!

Freeing Your Heart

Wow. You certainly have a lot of things. Maybe these items seemed exciting in the store or on TV, but once you brought them home and tossed them into a pile with all the other crap you've already amassed, you suddenly found yourself buried alive. Your job is to recognize that you're still alive under all that stuff! You can stand up. Movement in a positive direction has a way of knocking down walls. This is about breaking free, about breathing again. I'll help you decide what is important in your life. Your powers of discrimination will return.

Society and others tend to dictate what should be important in your life. That's why you have so much clutter — there are so many conflicting opinions bombarding you every day, so many things you think you need to keep, depending on whom you ask. Imagine the space that this excessive information takes up on your heart's hard drive. No wonder you keep crashing! Now *you* get to decide what really matters to you. Clutter busting frees up your heart. Imagine the powerful energy that lies in store once you start making up your own mind. Other people's opinions of your life don't matter. What matters is that *you* care about your life.

Human beings are brought up to fit in. It can be difficult to speak up at times — you don't want to upset the balance.

But remember, it helps to know that people love to be distracted by your life. It allows them to avoid taking care of their own. Only what *you* feel is important. You are the expert on your life. It's time to live comfortably amid the things that matter to you.

The Secret

Things will not make me happy. Repeat this phrase many times.

We try to give our lives significance by filling them up with things. But it just doesn't work. You never feel there is enough. By discarding things that are important to others but not to you, you start to live more spontaneously, and your natural joy comes through. Now is the time to be self-reliant. Now is the time to let go.

Hanging on to things is a way to avoid change. Change is inherent in every cell of your body. It occurs every second of your life. Nothing stands still. You can pretend change is not happening by distracting yourself with things that don't matter. But that doesn't suit you. You've been anesthetizing yourself with things to create a false sense of stability; meanwhile, change is going on inside and around you all the time.

When you begin to let go of the old useless artifacts of your past, you accept change, and you discover a profound peace of mind because you are going with the flow of life. There's momentum and power in that. That feeling of personal mightiness replaces the need to acquire things. Many of us own things to suppress feelings that we find difficult to face. But you cannot permanently suppress them. Now is the time to let those things go. The world misses you while you're in hiding. Come out. It is safe.

What Is Clutter Busting?

I clutter bust for a living. I sit down on the floor with total strangers in their homes and help them sort through their belongings. I ask them the questions they never think to ask themselves. "Do you need this, or can we let it go?" "When was the last time you used this?" "Do you like this, or can we let it go?"

It's funny. My clients often ask me for permission to toss their things. They paid for their things, they own them, they can do with them as they like. But they are scared to let go of something useless because they have been taught that it has some kind of value, and that "having things" in and of itself is valuable.

Once they let go of a few items, it becomes very freeing. They begin to comprehend the process and start tossing things before I even get a chance to ask them questions. *You possess the ability to let go.* Perhaps you haven't used this ability in a while, so it needs a little warming up.

The other day I got a call from a woman who was present at a clutter busting talk I gave to a business group. She told me afterward that she had gone to see her grandson soon after the talk. When he asked her what clutter busting was, she told him, "It's when people let go of the things they no longer need in their life." This little boy then went to his toy chest and separated out the toys he no longer played with. He told his grandmother that since he didn't use them anymore, he wanted them to go to kids who didn't have any toys.

Anyone can clutter bust. I used to be a slob. When I was a kid, I lived in a haze of dirty clothes, *Mad* magazines, and records lying out all over my bedroom floor. My mom had to yell at me to clean up my mess. But this made me more determined to continue in my cluttered ways. Things changed when I went to college and studied art. I was told by my instructors that it's important to have a clean work surface so your mind is clear to create great art. I had never thought of that. I tried it and found that when my art space was clean, it was easy to access unlimited creativity — I wasn't distracted. It felt good.

I became curious to see if having a clean space in other areas of my life would have a similar effect. I wanted my entire life to be art. I tried an experiment in my dorm room — I cleaned it. I picked up the tall pile of dirty clothes and whittled away at a former tree: the paper stacked on my desk. I even found a vacuum cleaner. I had never used one in my life. It sucked up all the food and dust and mystery items. There were loud clicking sounds as the vacuum gobbled them up. The first thing I noticed was that it felt good to be there, and that my room no longer smelled. My mind was peaceful. My usual worries were gone. There were no fires to put out. Everything was okay.

My next step on the road to clutter busting was a moving job I had in college. I became amazed at the amount of crap people haul from home to home. I couldn't see why people needed so much stuff. After all, a person can only use one thing at a time. It made me wonder why people don't just rent things when they need them. A lot of stuff looked old. Many things were scratched, dented, or torn. I found myself thinking that if the person I was moving found these things on the curb they would drive right by them. Sometimes people would still be packing when we arrived. They were frantically and indiscriminately grabbing everything and anything and throwing it into the nearest open box. There was no care in the packing of their items. So I figured they didn't care for their things. It seemed that the point was just to have things, that it would be a bad thing to have an open space.

People's things seemed to be a distraction of sorts, as though their possessions kept them from feeling some kind of sadness or pain. Many times there was an undercurrent of unexplored feelings, a nebulous sort of coveting. Another amazing thing I noticed was that the people we moved were typically very anxious. Couples would be yelling at each other. Some looked pale, tense, and fearful. I had a feeling that it was because deep down, they knew they had too many things and that a lot of it was worthless. People can be so tied to the worth of their things that they forget they have each other.

I remember asking one guy what was in some old-looking sealed boxes. He told me he didn't know. They had been with him since his last two moves. I said we ought to open them and find out. He got angry and told me to forget about it and just pack the boxes. I realized then that many people have a clutter problem and that they don't know where to begin to sort it out.

My next clutter epiphany came after college when I would visit my friends at their apartments, and they would anxiously warn me at the door that their places were a mess. I used to think, "If it bothers you that much, why don't you clean it?" Often I would end up helping them put their places in order. Afterward I noticed powerful and positive changes taking place in their lives. I began to realize that people don't know how to get rid of the things they no longer need. Most of us have a huge desire to acquire things. The problem is, we don't know when to stop, and we don't know how to toss. We never stop and think, "Why do I need this?" or, "What do I really want?"

Having so many things makes it hard for us to think clearly, which in turns makes it hard for us to be discriminating about our belongings. I experienced this in a profound way back in college, as I was starting to help my friends clear their spaces. I wanted them to have the peace of mind and joy that I had in my life. I noticed that my friends had strong feelings for many of their belongings. They knew these items were useless, but they kept a tight grip on them. When I began to ask them questions about the things, they loosened their grip. They began to see that many of their things lacked value. They had never looked at their possessions in this way. They had rarely looked at what was really important to them.

You know the feeling yourself. You currently own things that seem very important to you. If someone broke into your house and took them, you would most likely be devastated by the loss.

But what are you actually losing? Something *society* placed a value on? Something an ad tricked you into thinking would make you a better and happier person? Do things make you happy and stable, or do they cover up a scared and vulnerable feeling that you would rather not feel? How valuable are these things in your life?

We rarely ask these questions. Instead, we hang on to everything we own, and we even want more! We do this to feel better, but the action actually obscures the reality. We lose track of what really matters to us. The more possessions we gain, the more we lose. I discovered this in my own life, and I saw it with the people I helped move. I saw it with my friends whose ways I helped change. And that's why I started clutter busting: to help you let go of the things that no longer matter to you so you can truly begin to enjoy your life.

I don't want you to have to wait any longer to smile, to feel good about your life, to feel fulfilled, to feel that you are enough. Right now. To stay mired in your past, in the objects and career and people you have surrounded yourself with, is an old habit. Many of the things in your life are actually worthless to you. By reading this book, you will train your eye to see what is truly valuable. When I enter clients' homes, I assume that 75 percent of their things are no longer useful to them. I wrote this book to help you root out the extraneous, the superfluous, in your life, the things that have cluttered your hearts and lives, to help you figure out what *you* care about, to take your life back. Think of it as weeding the garden of your life. Isn't your garden a joy to behold after it has been freshly weeded?

Letting Go of the Past

Perhaps you are feeling some trepidation as you read these words. So let's pause for a moment to explore those feelings. When you think about clutter busting your home or office, do you fear losing your link with the past? If so, remember that the past doesn't matter. It's of no use to you now. The only proof of the past is in your memory — which has left out many details to support its beliefs and, along with a few bits of facts, has mixed in a pretty big dose of fantasy. Memory is very unreliable. When you hang on to your past, you are gripping an anchor that is swiftly moving to the bottom of the ocean. Sure, you have something to hang on to, but you are drowning too.

I once asked a friend of mine to go through the clutter-busting process with me. I told her what questions to ask and gave her permission to be relentless. When my friend found some of my old poetry and asked about it, I automatically replied, "It's important to me; it stays." She pursued me with questions and made me realize that I had handwritten and then typed them up ten years ago and had never looked at the poems since. I knew it was clutter. The poems had remained in a box for three moves. I was behaving exactly like some of the people I used to help move. I couldn't believe I was now guilty of this behavior! Still, I wanted to hang on to the poetry.

That's how powerful clutter can be. My friend asked me more questions about the poems. I maintained that they were really good writing; how could I throw them out? But

I realized that I had written these poems about relationships that had gone bad and about my sadness at the time. When I started to read a few, I felt old sorrows return. I had to ask if I wanted that in my life anymore.

I realized that a part of my heart was still holding on to some of those old relationships. I recognized my ingrained beliefs that "love is hard to come by" and that "I should hold on to whatever comes, even if it's painful and damaging." This was inner clutter causing the outer clutter. I didn't want to live with that extremely limited way of seeing the world anymore. I also knew that I couldn't ask my clients to let go of their clutter if I couldn't let go of mine. I tossed out the books. When they hit the trash can, they sounded like lead. The books had an emotional heaviness that became even more apparent when I let them go. I immediately felt free. I felt great relief in my heart — a feeling of expansiveness, the thing I was craving in the poems.

I observed that my attachment to the books, which had only a second ago been quite strong, was now gone. The books were now just old paper. This is a feeling my clients experience right after letting go of something they had felt was of great importance. The strong link to the *thing* had disappeared for good.

Believe it or not, just an hour after I tossed the poems, I got a call from CBS 2 News in Los Angeles. They wanted to do a feature story on my clutter-busting business. They had contacted me six months earlier, and now suddenly they had decided that I would make a good story. I felt this was connected to my having let go of the poems and my old beliefs. There was now room for something new and fresh and valuable in my life.

What is getting in the way of your experiencing powerful and necessary change? What have you made yourself believe is important that really isn't? What are you clutching that actually has you in its clutches?

You can let the past go.

You can already feel your fingers loosening their grip on your things.

Boy, it's nice to feel ease and relaxation seeping back into your awareness and joints. You are already starting to feel stronger and more able. Positive change will occur now that you are starting to let things go internally and externally.

Let go of expectations. When your life changes, it becomes something you've never experienced before. Therefore, you can't anticipate what it will be. Treat change like an unexpected present, one that comes wrapped in a box, and you have no idea what's inside. Let the words in this book infuse your heart. Lasting and profound change happens spontaneously. Let go of remembering. Follow the directions your heart will give you.

So let's get started. Here's how we'll proceed.

How This Book Is Organized

Right from the start I help you understand that clutter is anything in your life that no longer serves you. A closer inspection of your relationship to your things brings this understanding home. It's as if a spotlight begins to illuminate the clutter in your life.

In each chapter I give you pointers on how to take a closer look at your clutter. You'll see how you invest yourself in your things, and how you hide in your stuff to protect yourself from change. You'll become aware of how clutter keeps you stuck and living in the past and prevents you from living in the richness of *right now*. You'll discover how your need for clutter is an addictive tendency, and that it manifests from your inner clutter to keep you from feeling pain. By seeing the mechanics of how clutter operates within and around you, you'll gain a powerful understanding of your life. This understanding will give you clarity, which is your essential nature. As you begin to gain insight, your discriminating faculties come to life. You'll feel a burning desire to toss your clutter.

I'll share insights about what clutter is and how it affects your life as well as amazing stories about the people whose living spaces I helped to clutter bust. You will see that you are not the only one living with extraneous crap! The stories will further inspire you to find and toss your own unnecessary stuff. I've also provided you with some fun exercises to do. They are designed to help you loosen up and let go of your clutter. Think of them as a jump-start. Please feel free to improvise off any of them and, especially, to create your own. At the end of the book you'll find a Summary of Clutter-Busting Principles, to turn to whenever you need some inspiration in your tossing efforts.

The great thing about clutter busting is that it has a life of its own. Once you start, the momentum takes over. Stay with the process and feel your life open up. Your potential will be released. You will learn how to keep your life clutter free, ensuring that you will always stay open, bold, and beautiful.

Start by reflecting on what's in front of you now.

Chapter One

YOU ARE SACRED — YOUR THINGS ARE NOT

There is no inherent value in things. Things themselves are neutral, but we ascribe them false value. Things will never make you happy. Nothing, even the most beautiful piece of art, is sacred, except you. When you take care of yourself, you are happy. When you are happy, you don't need anything. You are content. Your life is satisfying. You're not compelled to acquire things to make you happy. You are already enough as you are.

If you are unhappy and you buy something to help you feel better, you are buying into an ad campaign that was designed to part you from your money. You are still unhappy, though temporarily distracted by the thing. When the newness wears off, you feel bad again. This is usually the point at which you acquire something new in an attempt to feel better.

Stop. Add nothing new at this point.

Drop the habit and come back to *you*. You are enough. You'll see.

Happiness is not an object. It is a subjective state. It is not dependent on things.

Once you start letting go of the clutter that you brought into your home as a distraction, you'll notice yourself becoming very calm. What you were looking for was there all the time — just buried under stuff.

You Need Nothing

You are born with nothing, and you will die with nothing. While you're alive you grasp things hoping they will improve you as a person, give you pleasure, make you win, get you attention. Grasping is a symptom of anxiety — intuitively you know that nothing gives lasting pleasure, that nothing is eternal. You know that things break, lose their luster, or get lost or stolen.

Imagine that you are drowning in the ocean. You are grasping at the objects floating past you to keep afloat. You grasp something, and it slips out of your hand, or you swim toward something and it floats out of your reach. You think it's all over. You are going to sink to the bottom of the ocean and drown. You give up.

But you don't sink. You float. You are able to stay on the surface without anything to assist you. It's a peaceful feeling. You are self-reliant. You don't need anything. You thought you did, but you were wrong. The panic is gone. The anxiety has dissolved. You feel true happiness at just being alive.

This is freedom from clutter. You really don't need anything. It was pure superstition to think otherwise. As you are, you are self-sustaining. This is the place that beauty and joy and love and excitement and adventure emanate from. When you are naturally fulfilled, you can finally enjoy life *right now*. The neediness that drove you to endlessly acquire and hold on to things was insatiable. Trying to satisfy it through shopping, surface relationships, and misguided attempts at success, manipulation, and control only made you feel worse.

Break the chain of thinking that things will make you happy. When you look closely, you see that they never did or that they gave the illusion of doing so only for a few seconds. Actions based on that hunger only made you even hungrier for more things. The momentum of living that way can be stopped. You can turn it around. When you think about it, it feels impossible. But when you take action, the momentum carries you forward. There's tremendous power in action. Your action, when strongly directed, breaks the inertia of sorrow and depression.

Reading this, you are already turning around. You are changing in a way that is natural to you. Lean in that direction. It will give you what you need. And it will keep giving you that freedom and peace and happiness. Out of habit, the mind may fret about the change. Keep letting go.

Desire

Like all of us, you feel low at times. Maybe you turn to a common solution to help you feel better right away: shopping. It doesn't matter if it's online or at the mall. You felt bad and wanted to cheer yourself up. You remembered all the ads you saw on TV or in magazines in which someone got some product and felt so much better, or you remembered something from your past that cheered you up and you wanted that thing again. You want to be that happy. Now.

But you weren't thinking clearly when you were out buying. So whatever you bought was flawed. It's not going to be something you need. Things do not contain the ingredients to make you happy. If you're feeling bad, maybe you need to reflect on your life, take it easy, and be nicer to yourself. Slowing down and reflecting can help change your state of mind. And it's free! You will not get a Visa card statement for it a month from now. I'm not saying that we can't buy ourselves new shoes if we need them, or that treating ourselves from time to time is not okay. Rather, this is about becoming more deeply aware of what is truly essential in the moment.

Another way to reflect is to think of a time when you absolutely had to possess some object. You felt a rush of excitement just thinking about having it. It was almost painful not to have this thing. When you got it, suddenly there was fulfillment and joy. The joy came not from getting the object but from the relief of letting go of the pain of wanting. When a terrible pain ends, isn't there great joy? This comes from the gratitude for the ceasing of pain.

Watch your experience of wanting something. Really feel it — it's uncomfortable. You feel things will not be okay until you have the item. Then be aware of how you feel when you get the thing. The needing subsides. There is peace of mind. *Getting* the thing didn't give you joy. The happiness comes from calming your mind. Advertising and misguided memories create your mind-set of wanting and needing. The desire is created through amazingly powerful psychological manipulation. You have been hypnotized into a state of pain, and the antidote is revealed to you: the object for sale. "This object will alleviate your suffering."

But you are complete and happy as you are. The *idea* of terrible lack was introduced into your awareness by ads and unhappy people — maybe you — and suddenly you felt terribly incomplete and had to resolve it. That's why it's hard to get rid of things: you bought the item thinking it would make you *better*. If you get rid of it, you think you're losing something that makes you a better person. But that's a mirage. You're doing better than you think.

Only Your Peace of Mind Is Sacred

I'm effective at clutter busting because I believe that *nothing is sacred except your happiness and peace of mind*.

You come to me with two things: complaints about your life and extreme attachment to your things. You have convinced yourself that everything you have is of value to you. Your attachment to the clutter keeps you from seeing its harmful effects. But remember: things are functional. Their job is to make your life easier or to increase your level of fun. Things become clutter when they no longer achieve either of those results. If you keep them, you are then working for your clutter. You work hard to pay the mortgage or rent so you can have a place to store your clutter. You are overwhelmed.

Since you are now my client, I'm going to help you sort out the nonessentials so you can let them go and simplify your life. Simplicity is happiness.

First ask yourself, What is most valuable?

Nothing is irreplaceable, except your peace of mind. It's your best asset.

You may feel that something you own is irreplaceable. But that's because you've told yourself it is.

What if you never owned it?

What if you never heard of it?

What about the things you don't own now?

What's important to you?

What's essential to you?

Watch kids play. Often they will forfeit expensive toys and make up games out of sticks or paper or simply play make-believe. You've been tricked into believing that expensive toys are more fun. Become a child again.

Your Home Is Like a Fridge

To become open to your life again, start by taking an honest look around. The following analogy will help you focus your awareness.

You have food in your refrigerator. Some of it might be spoiled. It was once fresh, but over time it went bad. The spoiled food makes the fresh food seem spoiled. So you go out to eat. Your home is like a fridge. The stuff inside is both fresh and spoiled. The fresh things are the items that still suit your life, things that are useful and make your life better. The spoiled things are items that you don't need or use. They take up space and become stagnant. They may have been spoiled when you brought them home, or maybe they were fresh and went bad over time. The spoiled stuff spoils your life, so you find excuses to leave the house; you may never even want to be home. Or you spend a lot of time at home, depressed and confused. Now is the time to toss the spoiled stuff and start enjoying your life. This is about taking care of *you*.

Do You Have Enough for Three People?

But it can be hard to take care of yourself when you're inundated with stuff. Even though we never even use most of our things, many of us desire even more. "If I had the DVD player... If I had the Lexus... If I just had the partner and a baby... then I'd be happy."

In the future we will be able to own an entire store. Whenever we feel lonely or depressed, we'll go to our store, pick something out of the thousands of items, and take it home. Then we'll come back an hour later. Well, the future is now. Stores give the illusion that they are there for you. "Whatever you need, come and get it. We're so happy to stay open for you." That's essentially how company websites operate. If things actually made a big difference in your life, you wouldn't need very much. You'd buy something and feel great for a very long time. When you're honest with yourself, you realize you never get a lasting feeling from any item.

That is because your life has meaning, and the things in your life don't. Visit a garage sale. The stuff there used to mean a lot to the person selling it. Rather than tossing or donating it and quickly moving on, they're now trying to give it away for fifty cents. In some ways, this is an attempt to show that the item is still worth something to them.

Anything can seem valuable to you. But that's only the meaning you place on it. It was your choice to give it value. The value is in your imagination. You fuel it with your grip. Hey, at one time you believed in Santa Claus.

Perspective is freedom. It's right now.

Clutter Is Inorganic

Before I started clutter busting, I used to bartend. I would go to people's homes and make drinks for their parties. One guy was throwing a big bash for his best friend's birthday, and many guests were in attendance. This guy had a huge, expensive sound system, and he was preoccupied with getting the music just right. The guests didn't notice. They were busy talking with one another.

It came time to light the birthday candles. The guy's wife told everyone to go to the living room for the event. The guy said he'd be right there, but he kept fiddling. I could hear all the action in the living room. People were applauding the cake. The guy's wife called to him from the other room to come join her, "right now." The guy called back that he'd be right there. I could hear the reaction to the candles being blown out. Then the guests drifted back into the bar area. The guy was still fixing the sound system. The wife was very angry with her husband. He ignored her.

This is a great example of how people get fixated on things that don't contribute to their well-being. They get caught up in clutter. They don't even recognize what they are doing or why. I'm willing to bet that most of your life is caught up in this kind of activity in one form or another.

The things that move and inspire you are fertilizer. They make your life blossom. Clutter, however, is inorganic. Nothing grows from its existence — not anything we can love, that is. One day we end up looking at all the crap we've accumulated and sadly realize we are barely alive in an infertile field.

Loosen your grip on the meaningless. Take to the open road — who knows where it will lead?

Placing Clutter Higher Than You

Here is a good example of becoming so invested in material things that we don't notice when their value has long expired. One of my clients had a photo of a man on her dresser. I felt compelled to ask who he was. She smiled and told me it was her guru, saying, "He is amazing!" On the floor next to her dresser was a pile of old dirty clothes. Under the clothes were some papers. When I picked them up, they felt emotionally heavy. They were clutter.

When I asked her about the papers, she turned pale and breathed deeply. She didn't want to look at them — another clue that they were clutter. After some questioning, she told me they were from a yoga course she took a year ago. The photo on her dresser was of her teacher. I asked her if the papers were important to her, or could she let them go. She looked pensive and seemed burdened. She confessed to me that she was not very spiritual; she felt she could never be good enough.

I asked, "According to whom?" It was odd for her to hear this. She was not used to questioning an unhealthy belief.

She said, "According to the course." She said that everyone in the class did really well but her.

I said, "According to your comparison of yourself to other people in a class — according to some paper and questions arranged by that guy — according to your assessment of the way a few other people live, you have decided to feel crappy about your life."

She looked relieved, so I continued, "You're feeling down because you are trying to shape your life in a way a few others are attempting to live rather than letting yourself intuitively decide what is appropriate for you. The only real spirituality is letting yourself flow — naturally, in tune with your innate abilities." I told her she would only lose herself if she compared herself to others and that her pain came from trying to force a lifestyle dictated by others.

I watched as she recognized her clutter. She threw the papers in the recycling bin, and then she threw out the photo of the guru. She looked light and happy. She was beaming. She had made space for her heart to expand, and it did.

As you look at your things, notice when something makes you feel cramped or tired or when it drags you down. What does it do to your energy? Is it holding you back? Ask what significance you've given the thing. Often by asking and being open, you can define an object's worth to you. If it has no value to you, toss it. Now.

Chapter Two

WE ASSUME FALSE IDENTITIES IN CLUTTER

You have an addiction. You are hooked on identifying with your things, on seeing them as representative of who you are.

If you are like many people, then you tend to identify with the labels associated with things: jobs, hobbies, whether you are married or single, and personal habits (you're a smoker, a nonsmoker, an early bird, a night owl). But those things aren't *you* because you are constantly changing. Yet you are addicted to describing what you are. That's why it's hard to let go of the things, the labels. If you really looked at who you are, without the professional and personal nouns, you would see that by nature you are very simple. Who you really are requires no support. You can enjoy things, but you don't need them.

You're doing better than you think you are. You are a unique brand — a unique identity.

Tossing Out Self-Blame

If you are feeling ashamed of your addiction, remember that your clutter situation is not entirely your fault. Billions of advertising dollars are spent every year to get you to feel that your life is worthless unless you buy things, whether or not you actually need them. You have been ambushed, continually, for years and decades.

What's the anatomy of an ad? A person is sad and lacks something. Suddenly a product is introduced into her life. The music gets louder and stronger, and the colors brighter. The actor portraying the person becomes happy.

When you are subjected to this thousands of times a year, you start to feel that "Things make me happy. Whatever I buy will change my life. Go, go, go out and get something, *now!*" You are driving somewhere — probably to buy something — and out of the corner of your eye you spot a billboard that plants a subconscious buying command in your brain. The same thing happens with magazines, product names on clothing, newspapers, designer labels, even movies with product placement ads. You are living in a society that has been programmed to think of buying as a way of life. You see everyone living this way, and you have not been taught to question this unsatisfying behavior.

It would be great if you bought something and you really were satiated. "Ever since I bought those shoes fourteen years ago I've been so happy. I've only bought food since." But you get something you don't really need, and then you're quickly bored. Advertising programming kicks

in, and you think, "I'll feel much better if I just get _____."
You reminisce about how something made you feel once,
and you go out and buy it again. The cycle doesn't end until
you stop and recognize this pattern — which you're doing
right now.

It can often be hard to stop this cycle because ads prey
on your desire for emotional stability. "You can have the
love and health and security you desire if you own this
thing." But in life there is no permanent stability. Things
are constantly changing. Maybe you can imagine there is
permanence, but you have been brainwashed.

And advertising is a great brainwasher. Scenarios pre-
senting the point of view that "things will make you happy"
have been ingrained into your belief system. A belief system
is an unconscious psychological function that structures how
you see and react to the world. Because you are unaware of
it, it remains unquestioned. As a result, you look automatically to things to bring you happiness, which the things
don't, *won't*, and *can't* do. This makes you unhappy and psychologically unstable because something that is supposed to
be true is not happening. You blame yourself. You don't
examine your belief system and instead continue to acquire
things. The cycle doesn't end because you haven't looked
at the root cause of what is happening. The only way out is
to walk away. Walk away from things. Let go of what the
world of advertising tells you is the right way.

Things do not help you maintain your well-being;
rather, they keep you from seeing what you really need and
want in your life. When you start to toss the junk out of your

life, the veil lifts. You see the ever-changing nature of life, and in your heart you accept this constant change. Once this happens, you're happy because you've finally become free from a lie.

Are You Living a False Life?

If you are like other people, you have been living a false life — an image, concept, brand that you picked up. Unconsciously, you felt it would improve you in other people's eyes. And once you were accepted by others, you thought you would finally accept yourself.

Other people have a strong influence on you. You make yourself into something you are not to get others' approval. You live in constant fear that even if you do win their approval, at any second they could still change their minds. Gasp!

What can you do with approval? Nothing.

Most people live for approval, but it doesn't make them happy. There are lots of miserable people. Your need to impress others and get their approval is a losing battle and causes you to acquire clutter. What will help you let go of this obsession is the recognition that *most people are obsessed with getting approval and being accepted*. They really don't care about your life. They want your acceptance of their life.

The people you so badly want approval from want your approval.

Look at the president of the United States. He or she is supposed to be the most powerful person on earth. Many are trying to get this person's approval. But those at the White House take public opinion polls to help them make the right decisions so the president can get reelected. The president needs *your* approval. And in the second term he worries about legacy, how he will be seen by history.

You will never feel there is enough approval, so you will never approve of yourself. Living this way is clutter. It adds nothing to our lives but grief and sorrow. You will never feel accepted enough. But *self*-acceptance is enough.

In fact, it is everything. Your life settles when you feel you are enough. Who you really are, the stripped-down version of you, is the only place where you have power and freedom.

You've Become What You Own

Often, because you don't feel like you are enough as you are, you start to identify with what you own, whether it's your car, your CDs, or your furniture. That's why you get upset when something you own is stolen or breaks, and that's why you're okay if it happens to someone else. Combine that with the advertising trance that's caused you to place too much value on *things*, and it becomes difficult to let go.

Where your attention goes, so spreads your life force. Where you put your energy and attention, you leave your mark. In a deep way, what you currently own has your mark, your scent. You can break these bonds when you use your powers of discrimination and honestly question whether something in your life has value or is in your way.

When you do this, the identification, the familiarity, drops away. It's no longer personal. It is no longer "mine."

Simply reading this book will help you begin to remove clutter from your life. You are removing clutter even now, as you are turning these pages.

Secret Stashes

A woman I worked for a few years ago was holding on to clutter that supported her belief that she was not enough as she was. She had secret stashes of spiritual self-help audio cassettes. They were so well hidden that she'd even surprise herself when she'd come across them. I'd open a drawer and begin an excavation and suddenly, under a bunch of miscellaneous clutter, I'd find another batch of them. There were tapes tucked into the back of cupboards and drawers and under the bed and in boxes in her garage and in the back of closets. There were hundreds of them. My client couldn't avoid buying them — she purchased them compulsively. Many of the tapes were unopened, and many were duplicates.

She was embarrassed about having these tapes. She felt that her need for them was a sign of weakness and that she should be strong and capable enough to make the right decisions on her own. Instead she had to rely on people she had never met who whispered their wisdoms into a microphone.

She revealed that her desire to be a "better person" was fueled by a need for others to see her as being good enough.

I said, "You can only feel good about yourself when everyone else feels you're good enough? That's a pretty impossible obstacle you've set in front of yourself."

She cried. A lot. When you hear your beliefs spoken out loud, often you can release them. Just imagine the strain of her cluttered, harsh thinking; she was exhausted. After wiping away the tears, she seemed twenty years younger. She was smiling. The inner clutter, which was causing the outer clutter, had been removed.

She put all but two tapes in a box for donation, and these two she left out in the open on her dresser. I didn't even ask her to do that. This meant that these particular tapes were no longer clutter and were now of benefit to her.

EXERCISE

- Take a look around. Do you have a lot of duplicate items in your home?
- Ask yourself, "What do I get by keeping these items? Do I really want them in my life? Am I keeping them for me, or for someone else?"

I work with a lot of "successful" clients whose inner drive to succeed takes a huge toll on them physically and psychologically. They have installed a program in their minds that is working against them. The appearance of their success has become more important than how they are feeling.

Do you have this kind of clutter in your life?

- Complete this statement: "I am successful when _____."

> - Is this *your* version of success or someone else's?
> - Does it make you happy? Can it ever?
>
> By asking these questions, I'm getting you into the habit of asking what's really valuable to *you*. Looking at what you value and how you think and make decisions helps you to look honestly at the things in your life. You will find it easy to remove the clutter, weed the garden, and live a life that bears the fruit of *you*.

Expensive Clutter Is Still Clutter

Sometimes people value something merely because it was expensive. Here's an example. A middle-aged couple hired me to help them clean out their garage. What stood out immediately was a very large collection of sporting equipment: skates, both four-wheel and inline; camping equipment; skis; basketballs; footballs; ski machines; a trampoline; a Pilates machine; a badminton set; a stationary bicycle; and a rowing machine.

These things were stacked one on top of another as if they were in a junkyard (clutter loves to cling to other clutter). When I asked the couple when they had last used the items, they couldn't remember. "Perhaps a couple of years ago." When I suggested they could let it go, they replied that that would be impossible, because it had cost them a lot of money.

I said, "I would think if you spent a lot of money on something that you don't use, you'd want to get rid of it so you wouldn't feel bad that you'd wasted your money every time you saw it."

They didn't say anything. I asked them if they exercised. They told me they hiked in the hills behind their home every evening with their dogs and that hiking was their favorite activity of the day. They looked forward to it. They were happy and animated when they talked about this activity.

I suggested that maybe hiking was good enough for them, and they agreed. I said, "When you thought about the sports clutter in your garage you looked pained and confused. You seemed weak, lost, and guilty. You were punishing yourselves. When you talk about hiking, you get animated and energetic and happy. You're healthy because of it. Which one of these states of physiology do you want on a regular basis?"

I could see in their eyes that they got it.

The woman said, "So it's okay if we just toss the sports stuff?" I got on the phone right away with a charity organization and set up a pickup time for all the equipment. With the decision made, the couple radiated peace.

We often place value on something because it cost a lot of money rather than because it brings us fulfillment and happiness. We identify with the price tag or the brand name and forget to notice if the stuff actually makes us happy. Happiness is straightforward and simple. It doesn't need an explanation. If you find yourself overdefending an object, then you know it's clutter.

- Ask yourself, "What have I bought that I'm not using?" Perhaps it's some kind of electronic device that was supposed to make your life easier. Maybe it is a book that was recommended to you or that you thought could help transform your life. Perhaps it's some clothing you bought on a whim.

- Put that object in a new place in your home. If you don't use it in this new place, or if you decide to wait until later, then it's clutter. If you're using it and it feels heavy and you want to stop using it, it's clutter. If you're using it and you get a feeling of glee and joy and openness, it stays.

- Place the item on a table or chair. Imagine that it's in a courtroom, and the object is on the witness stand. Ask it to swear to tell the truth, the whole truth, and nothing but the truth.

- Ask the item if it should go. Honesty comes in yes or no answers. Further elaboration is just a delay in getting to the truth. Ask yourself what you would prefer to use instead. Find out what you really want to do.

Affirmations as Clutter

My client was the pastor at her church. She considered it her job to inspire her congregation. She hired me because she needed some help with her office. Her desktop was overflowing. All kinds of books and papers were piled under and around the desk. They gave the appearance of a huge life preserver that kept the desk from sinking.

I noticed affirmations taped to the wall surrounding her desk. There were more than twenty of them. "I am becoming a better person every day." "I am learning to be a loving soul." "I am becoming the person God wants me to be." The paper was turning yellow and curling. Some had fallen behind the desk. These affirmations had been up there a long time, and they were doing a lousy job of affirming. They seemed to be mocking her, acting as harsh reminders of what she was not. I took them off the walls and put them on the floor. I read them out loud. I told her she didn't need to have these up anymore, that she'd already achieved the stated goals.

I said, "You're already a good person. You don't have to prove it to yourself anymore. You are more than enough. If you actually saw what you are now, you'd be a lot happier. You don't need something outside you to remind you of why you make a difference."

She nodded and cried. She bent down with a decisive vigor and crumpled up the pieces of paper and tossed them in a recycling bin. It was easy to clutter bust her desk after this. Within a few hours her office was clean and orderly.

Sometimes clutter, like my client's affirmations, can seem like a positive thing. But maybe having it in your life allows you to overidentify with something, in this case some ideals about how to be, because you don't feel good enough as you are. Time to toss.

Piles of Books

Here is another example of clutter holding its owner captive. I was hired by a woman for a general clutter-busting assignment. She lived in a studio apartment; her living room and bedroom were combined. Most of the room was filled by hundreds of books. The bookshelves covered most of the wall space. There was not even room for every book, and many were waiting in piles at the base of bookshelves. I joked that I didn't know she was a branch of the LA County Library. She laughed nervously. She knew it was a problem but had been afraid to admit her feelings.

She told me that she had OCD (obsessive-compulsive disorder). When I work with clients who tell me they have OCD, I let them know I've heard them, but I don't elaborate on it because I am not qualified to do so. In fact, I want to slow the thinking down and get them to the simple feeling level. I find that keeping the process simple and just coming back to "Do you need this, or can we let it go?" keeps the person in the moment and they forget about their situation and make good decisions. I've seen a lot of people with OCD or ADD (attention deficit disorder), some of whom are medicated, stun themselves with their ability to let go. I have also worked with people who have self-diagnosed themselves with OCD. They read about it and identified with it and used it as an excuse not to change. Many of these people are able to let go of things without further clinical assistance. However, if you think that you or someone you know has a serious disorder, please seek the advice of a mental health professional.*

I saw that the books were covered with dust, so I asked her how often she read. She said she'd been busy for a while and hadn't gotten around to doing any reading. She was grimacing, she looked pale, and her shoulders were hunched up. It was obvious she didn't like talking about her book situation.

I said, "Let's go through your books and see what we can let go."

She was hesitant but agreed.

My client hadn't read most of the books, but she wanted to. She wanted to hang on to them. She became defensive when I asked her why. I changed tactics. I asked what her books meant to her. She looked off, and her face glowed. She was in a trance. She looked like a little girl. She told me how powerful books are and how important knowledge is to her, how it's important to keep growing.

I heard anxiety in her voice. I realized her actions were

---

* You can learn more about compulsive hoarding in David F. Tolin, Randy O. Frost, and Gail Steketee, *Buried in Treasures: Help for Compulsive Acquiring, Saving, and Hoarding* (New York: Oxford University Press, 2007).

fueled by feelings of inadequacy, that she possessed an elusive goal of some high degree of intelligence. She unconsciously felt she could never be smart enough, but she was desperate to try. She was overwhelmed by this drive. She couldn't keep up and wanted to give the impression that she could — hence the books.

Does this sound familiar?

She was living amid clutter that enslaved her. These books didn't make her feel good. On the contrary, they were the absolute reminder of her number one belief: that she wasn't good enough.

Often people surround themselves with things that, on the surface, appear to make them more intelligent or interesting. They hope that people will be enamored by the glittery trappings and trophies and will believe they represent their owner, like some kind of placard. Many people do this with degrees and awards and big accomplishments and toys and even the people in their lives. Often people believe in their own hype.

When you clutter bust, question these things, awards, people. They will show what you are trying to avoid, which is usually centered on not feeling good enough, not feeling worthy. Our culture makes you try to prove your worth through what you've obtained and what you've accomplished. You then feel that once you attain these things (clutter), you will be good enough. Either you get these things and still feel like a miserable ass, or the goal is unattainable and you give up. Or you try to attain the goal and can't, proving to yourself that you're not good enough.

I wrote this book to tell you that the process of collecting stuff to beef yourself up is a lie. You're absolutely enough *right now*, regardless if you do this or that — or if you do nothing.

I said to my client, "You're more valuable than your books. You stand miles higher than all the volumes you have stacked up in here. Unless you believe that, you can own all the books in the world and still not feel smart enough."

She stayed silent as the words sank in.

My client told me that she wished people saw how smart she really is. She felt she couldn't do enough and that people didn't recognize her for her abilities. "I feel invisible."

I replied, "The people we try to impress are not good barometers. They are caught up in their own lives, trying to get others' approval. What matters is what you're thinking. You can build a great life from that foundation."

She said, "Okay, I'm ready." We began putting the books in boxes for donation to the local library.

EXERCISE

- Find an item that you haven't used in more than a year or that you've never used. Place it on a chair and sit across the room from it. Imagine that this clutter can talk. Start simply with small talk. Introduce yourself. Tell it about your day. Mention that you've had no interaction with it for a long time now and you're wondering why it's still here. Either intuitively hear what the thing has to say, or speak the item's words out loud. Whatever comes up is the truth. Accept the answer.

- Ask the item if it would now be okay if it went away. Sometimes things and people just want to be heard. If the answer is yes, thank it and let it go right then and there. If there's resistance, keep asking as if you're a newspaper reporter doing an interview.

Impartiality brings the truth. You'll know when you hit truth, because it will give you a feeling of peace and renewed energy.

Chapter Three

CLUTTER KEEPS US LIVING IN THE PAST

Do you try to trap feelings in the things you associate with those feelings? This practice is based on your belief that great moments are rare and need to be caught and preserved and incessantly recalled or saved for a rainy day. You have become unhappy with your life, so you have a great longing for the past. Living in the past brings emotional, psychological, and practical damage to your life because it prevents a focus on life *now*, which makes things seem even worse and creates an even stronger craving for the past. This is a downward spiral. By recognizing your past as moments that have lost their original vitality, you remove your attachment to it and allow yourself to flow spontaneously into the present, to get peace of mind, and to love your life just as it is.

Clutter Made of Memories

If you own something that you don't use and can't see yourself using, but you don't want to let go of it, what is happening? You are under the influence of the powerful emotional memories your mind associates with the thing.

The item is just a thing. It's neutral. There may be hundreds of thousands of this particular thing made by people in low-paying jobs. These people came to work every day and made this same exact thing in a robotic state of mind. Every one of these hundreds of thousands of the thing is exactly the same.

But you've embellished the thing through your memories and your attachment. You see it for more than it really is. You believe that if you toss it, you'll toss the joy you felt in your initial encounters with it. We're not talking about tossing the actual joy, just the *memories* of joy. Or the joy you thought you would get from the item. Those are the unfulfilled expectations that you're still waiting to get from the thing. These beliefs are based on fear. You're telling yourself that happiness is rare. You're saying, "It's probably not going to come to me again, so I'd better trap and protect this essence." This action makes you rigid. You close off the possibilities of other, richer kinds of happiness and fulfillment. If the thing really was a joy giver, why aren't you using it anymore? Why are you indecisive about tossing it? Because deep down you know it's lost its usefulness.

Being aware of this clinging, inflexible way of thinking helps you to let go. You're clutter busting the inner clutter, which is the source of all your outer clutter. You're getting rid of the root of your clutter.

Let's take an honest look at memories. A memory is a recollection of something that is no longer happening. It may have been bitter and sad, happy or pleasant, but the reality is, it's over. A memory is a vague representation, a shadow of the actual event.

Furthermore, most people's memories are inaccurate. People remember fragments of events and feelings, about a tenth of what actually happened. They don't remember anything completely. Certain aspects have been edited out, and fantasy elements have been added in. The mind is an imaginative tool — it's not reliable for objectivity.

When you hang on to something because of the emotional memories associated with it, your actions are based on a fictional reenactment of a real-life event. This is the primary reason my clients sometimes act oddly and give me strange answers when I ask them about certain items. Their memories come up.

If you're living off memories, you're on very shaky ground. You may crave the memories, but you're investing a lot of yourself in something that has *been* rather than on what *is*. To glorify and live saturated in the past is to live in your imagination. Your life will certainly suffer as a result. For when you get lost in the past, a gap is created between accepting what is happening and what you hope will happen. This could be behind your hesitation in tossing your clutter: to let go of things means to *let go* of desires for or dreams of a specific outcome. Let *go* of the item and stand on the solid ground of your life as it is right now!

Let Go of Expectations

Having expectations is another way we hold on to clutter from the past. Based on our past experiences, we expect and believe in a particular outcome. Our mind clings to this possible outcome as certain and necessary for our happiness. There is similar energy in the rigidness of the mind gripping an expectation and in a person hanging on to a thing that's no longer a part of his life. Expectations can end up becoming a great source of misery.

When you isolate and view the unconscious mechanics of expectation they turn out to be crazy: you wish, hope, predict, expect that out of innumerable possible outcomes of an event, *your* desired outcome will happen. It's similar to lottery odds. You don't get upset when you don't win the lottery, but most of us get upset when our expectations are not met. Hey, if you're demanding one outcome, you're going to be upset a lot. You're better off expecting that what you want to have happen won't happen. That way you'll be happy if it happens and happy if it doesn't. If you're expecting that this thing you're hanging on to will make you happy, *let go of the thing*.

You could use the peace of mind. Essentially, by being aware of the situation, really seeing it, really feeling the struggle, you will be able to drop your attachment to your things. Whether it's your intense grasp of memories or your expectations, your honest observation will help you loosen and relax the hold — like the sun evaporating a puddle.

You'd be amazed at how often I see people let go of old beliefs in an instant. That's why I encourage you so consistently and strongly. When clutter goes, you're left open to new and better experiences. Fresher ones. Things that are happening now. Would you eat lasagna that you cooked three years ago? Or would you rather have a fresh plate made and served right now?

I can smell something good baking in the kitchen.

Clutter Busting, Ghost Busting

Two of my clients were a married couple who had a multitude of framed photos hanging behind the headboard of their bed. There were pictures of their kids when they were much younger. None of the photos were of the kids as they were then, in their late-teenage years. There were a lot of pictures of dead relatives and of friends they didn't see anymore. And most of the photos were of other people. There were no pictures of themselves as a loving couple.

These were indications that they were stuck in the past, when things were "better," as they imagined them to be. Nothing in their bedroom signified or celebrated the life they were living now. Glorifying the past is the same as pretending you live in a stable world where things stay the same. It is easy to do. Just surround yourself with a lot of things that remind you of feelings you had during that time.

It is like being drunk or high. You buy something to give you a feeling that covers up what you are currently feeling. You overlay the present moment with a memory. It is a way of pretending that everything is all right. Meanwhile, the present suffers because your attention is not there. The longer you spend in the memory of the past, the further away you move from actual joy of *right now*.

Things change, even when you pretend they don't.

People wish this weren't true, even in the midst of big changes. That is why so many mood-changing medicines, like Prozac and Zoloft, are prescribed — to make everything seem okay. Staying stuck in memories is another form of virtual reality. It is simulated, a self-created fantasy world. This would be okay if the past made your life better. But it doesn't.

To the couple with the photos, I said, "Having your wall of photos is like living in a cemetery with the corpses strewn on the ground outside their graves. These are images of the dead past. You've got to have living things in your bedroom if you want to stay alive as a couple. Let's take these off the wall."

When we took all the photos down, there was just bare wall with dirt marks as borders to the new clean spaces. The feeling was profound — as if the room had been blabbing nonstop for ten-plus years and suddenly it was silent.

The couple too was silent. They were savoring the quiet. They hadn't felt this calm before. They were in awe.

I waited about a minute and then quietly asked, "Do you want me to put the photos back up?"

"No!"

Instead they decided to have the room repainted.

When I called the woman a week later, she told me that things had completely shifted in her marriage. They had not been getting along well for a few years, she told me. Now they were getting along like the best of buddies. The shift had been seamless. They decided to continue simplifying in other areas of their lives. The husband quit his high-stress job in an advertising firm and went to work as a freelance consultant for environmental protection companies, something he'd been talking about doing for years.

They had stopped living in the past and had stepped into the joyful present.

EXERCISE

- Bring a friend with you into your bedroom. Pretend that your bedroom is an art gallery and that your friend is a prospective buyer. Show her each item on your bedroom wall, and try to sell her the items. You'll know if an item has worth by the feeling of your sales pitch. Your friend will know it too.
- Let your friend actually buy something if she wants to. It's nice to make a little spending money!

EXERCISE

- Take an inventory of the nostalgia items in your home. These can be photos, camcorder cassettes, letters, trophies, clothes, newspapers, books, magazines, kitchen items, CDs, or movies. Nostalgia items are anything you own that gives you a strong connection to the past.

- Take the items from their space and bring them to one location. Hold each item. Feel what it gives you. Ask yourself, "Does keeping this make life better right now, or is this in the way of my finding new and better ways to explore life, love, and joy?" Be really honest with yourself. The mind can talk you into feeling anything. Beware of the safe, false feeling of the past. *The memories of joys in the past are miniscule compared to the joys you can experience in your life right now.*

  Past joys are memories, facsimiles of a moment. New moments are fresh, vibrant, and fulfilling. They give you the feeling of being alive that you are craving.

A Recipe for Clutter

I was hired by a woman who wanted me to help her clear out her garage. We went through her kitchen to get to the garage, and suddenly my clutter radar was activated. I looked toward her kitchen counter and saw a group of recipe books located just below the cupboards. On top and in between the books were pieces of paper that were crammed, stuffed, folded, and scrunched. When I asked what they were, she told me they were not important and kept walking toward the garage. I stopped and asked again. She became defensive and said, "Really, that's unimportant; they're just recipes."

I knew from her reaction that the heap of papers was clutter and that some heavy emotional clutter lurked behind the mess. When I took a look, I found a spasm of magazine and newspaper food recipes. I pulled the papers out of the clutter nest.

I asked if she cooked often. She told me she loved to cook but confessed she never had the time. She and her girls ate out at restaurants for every meal. When I asked her why she didn't cook, she looked like she might cry. She said that as a girl she had loved to cook, but then she got married. Her husband hated her cooking, and for eighteen years of marriage she cooked the same bland meals, things he would like, every day. She told herself she had to do what he wanted. There was deep resentment in her voice. For those eighteen years, she had saved recipes that she wanted to try, without ever trying them.

Though she had been divorced for two years, she still was not cooking. Her husband's powerful influence still swayed her. Both the recipes and her moratorium on cooking were clutter in her life. I told her we would go through all the recipes and pick the ones she wanted to try.

I carried the clump of recipes to the kitchen table, and we began to go through them. She was very vulnerable, and a few minutes into this, she began to cry. I told her this was good. It was her life now to do with what she wanted. At this she exploded into tears and cried hard for five minutes. When the tears subsided, we began going through more recipes.

She carefully considered each recipe, tossing some, keeping some. It became clear that she loved the art of cooking. She sprang right back into this love, which she had freely experienced when she was a teenager. The heaviness and the lines in her face were gone. She was radiating joy and freedom.

My client kept about a third of the recipes. We placed them neatly in a folder next to her cookbooks. She was in her element and decided to make me a salad from one of the recipes she kept.

It was delicious.

EXERCISE

Where are your recipes? The ones you really want to try, but haven't? Maybe you have the machinery in your house to do it, but you aren't using it. You pretend that having the thing is enough. But that's like having food in your fridge and not eating it. You've got to eat. You've got to have something in your life that you really care about and use with passion.

- Find an item in your home that you are not using. It may be a musical instrument that you have wanted to learn or a self-instruction book. Place it in a prominent place. If you don't use it in the next day or two, toss it.

Perhaps you don't yet know what you really care about and want to use with passion. By letting go of the clutter obstructions, you'll attain the clarity to know where to go next.

A Diva Tosses the Stuffed Animals

I was hired to clutter bust the home of a well-known singer. She was a strong-minded woman with a very messy apartment. The most intriguing thing in her place was her bedroom. She had more than fifty stuffed animals neatly placed in rows on her bed. There was no room to even sit or lie down.

I asked her how she slept with the zoo. She told me that she took all the animals off the bed at night, and in the morning she put them all back again. She revealed that they were given to her by different boyfriends. I figured they left them on the bed when they came over. I asked if she had a current boyfriend. With a tinge of sadness, she said, "No." She just couldn't seem to find one. I told her she would find one when she got rid of all the animals.

She was overwhelmed at the thought.

I said, "You are reminded of all your boyfriends when you have contact with the animals, when you remove them at night. You don't feel as lonely. But in a way, it only makes you lonelier because you remember them and then you go to bed all by yourself." She confirmed my assessment with her sad expression.

I told her she'd feel better when she let them go. She'd be opening herself up to opportunity. Plus, a lot of kids would get to play with the animals because I'd drop them off as a charity donation. She agreed. People will often transform when you're sweetly and directly honest with them. This also applies when you do the same for yourself.

As soon as I put the stuffed animals in a couple of plastic bags and removed them from the room, she looked relieved.

If you're trying to live with a lot of competing memories, they end up taking up space that would normally be reserved for peace of mind. You have an open-all-night Memory Festival going on in your heart and mind. It seems normal to you because there is no silence to contrast it with. People glow when they let go of clutter because they get that natural, silent peacefulness back.

The singer opened the clutter-busting floodgates by letting go of her boyfriend mementos. After we tossed the stuffed animals, she went to her closet and ended up letting go of a lot of her old clothing. She confessed that she had bought a lot of her clothes when she was feeling sad and lonely. She wanted to feel happy, and the advertising hypnosis kicked in and said, "You'll feel so much better when you go out to the stores and start buying. Trust me." If you're feeling down, you're not thinking clearly and you *will* purchase things that you will not like.

When she was done tossing, she actually looked thinner! This demonstrates how much emotional weight clutter adds to your physiology. There is a subtle body. It is the weight of emotions that sit stagnantly in the body when they are suppressed. These are "pounds" on a feeling level.

When you allow change to occur spontaneously and regularly in your life, your emotions flow through you like a fast-moving river. You will feel lighter, and others will notice your new "physique" too.

A Buried Marriage

A movie music writer hired me to clean out his music studio, which was in his home. He had a lot of old computer discs containing old music that he no longer needed. Other than that, the studio wasn't too cluttered. He started dropping hints about some items that needed to be filed in his office, so I asked to check out the office. It turned out it was located in his bedroom, which was a cluttered maze of overflowing boxes, tipped stacks of paper, and huge piles of clothing.

I told him we were done with the studio; the bedroom needed the most focus. The first thing I focused on was his sofa, which was covered with a tall clothing pile. When I asked him if he liked sitting on the sofa, he said he didn't care much for it. I asked if we could put it outside on the curb so that someone else could take it home and use it. He was excited at the idea that it was okay to do that. We took the sofa outside to the curb.

The next thing that caught my attention was his desk. It was an old wooden desk surrounded by unpacked boxes and covered with a web of papers. It felt like a sleeping dinosaur. I asked him if he liked the desk. He grimaced and said it used to belong to his father. He told me how his dad made a lot of money but never enjoyed his work or his money.

I said, "That's not your way." He nodded. "Let's get rid of the desk. You're better off starting fresh. It's time for you to stop living in your daddy's home and move into your own." We took the desk downstairs and put it next to the couch on the curb.

Next we began going through the papers. Most of them were extraneous and went right into a recycling bin. He was surprised to learn that he didn't need most of the papers. We filled up three bins. Toward the bottom of the last box, he found his marriage certificate. He told me he had been divorced for a year and looked forlorn. He had become deeply lost in his past. He had started looking like a very old man, even though he was only in his late twenties.

I told him there wouldn't be much use for the certificate, unless he wanted to remarry his former wife. He snapped back into the moment, tore up the certificate, and tossed it in the trash. He looked completely refreshed and much stronger than he had when I first showed up. Since the marriage certificate had been lying on the bottom of the deepest box, I knew the reason for his failure to unpack. He had to hold on to that much clutter to cover up the sadness he felt about his divorce.

I knew he'd be okay now. He was free from the clutches of the past. Being in the moment is the only stability you'll ever have in your life.

EXERCISE

Make a ceremony out of getting rid of your clutter. One of my clients once burned an entire garbage bag full of things an ex-boyfriend gave her. She told me it felt so good and it would not have felt nearly as good if she had merely tossed the stuff.

- You can do this ceremony if you have access to a fire pit or a fireplace and you have emotional attachment to clutter that is paper or wood. Place your clutter in the fire pit. Light it with a match or lighter. Watch the items burn as you feel relief knowing that these burdens from the past are no longer a part of your life. As the fire burns, you allow the past to fade and the present moment fills your heart again.

Clothes Storm

Another client tied to her past called to tell me about her "clothing situation." It seemed she had so many clothes in her apartment that she couldn't move around comfortably. When I went to her home, I saw that her clothing was everywhere. Rather than putting the clothes on hangers or stacking them in a dresser, she had draped them everywhere. There were clothes hung over books in the bookshelf. It looked like her apartment itself was clothed. This typically means someone is covering up some powerful feelings.

When I asked her how long her home had been like this, she told me ten years.

I got the image of her home as a cocoon. She was inside hoping one day to become a butterfly, something better. To me she already was a butterfly. She was having problems because she wouldn't allow herself to see who she was.

She had a huge, bonfire-size pile of clothes in front of her closet, blocking the closet from opening. When I asked her what was in the closet, she said more clothes, but she couldn't remember which ones.

The clothes also covered her tiny bed. When I asked her how she slept, she said she pushed the clothes to the end of the bed and curled up. There was an ironing board in the middle of the room. It was also layered with piles of clothing. I asked how she ironed. She told me that she hated ironing. That's why she piled her clothing on everything. She felt if the clothes weren't folded, they wouldn't need to be ironed.

When I suggested tossing some of the clothes, she balked and asked if we could simply organize them. I explained that her clutter had risen to the surface and was in her way. I told her that the longer she waited, the taller her piles would grow and the more she would start tripping over everything. "I want to help you give yourself a smooth, clear surface on which to live." She agreed.

We started with the pile in front of the closet. I went piece by piece, asking her many questions. "When was the last time you wore this? Do you still like it? Is it you? Would you buy it if you were out shopping today? Do you feel good when you wear it? Does it make you feel attractive? Or does it no longer fit? Can we let it go?" If she defended a piece of clothing with, "But it's in style," I'd ask, "But do *you* like it?"

Always come back to yourself when deciding what to keep or toss. Does the item make you feel good? Does it improve your life? Or have you been hanging on to it because of the memories associated with it?

Your life is not a museum. It is a living thing.

She got the idea, and we let go of many of her clothes.

People are generally very smart. Bad habits make their lives fall apart. She was adopting better habits and was already feeling the benefit. Next we cleared the way to her clothes closet. I opened the door. It felt like I was opening a clothes crypt. The door's hinges cracked and creaked. A strong musty smell escaped.

She was as curious as I as to what lay inside.

We found a lot of dresses. Many she associated with a man she had dated for five years, who had bought them for her. Their relationship had ended badly. When she spoke of the breakup, her emotional wounds were brought out into the fresh air of her awareness. Some part of her still cherished the relationship, and she was still in mourning, as if the man had died. We were visiting the graveyard of that relationship. She had unconsciously barricaded the entrance to this crypt with clothes, but the ghosts still got out and had been haunting her for years.

I told her, "You started covering up your feelings by creating this pile of clothes in front of the closet, and it grew to cover your entire place."

That's the thing about suppressing your emotions: when you do it in one place, it extends everywhere. By keeping yourself from feeling a big emotion, you shut down your feeling-discriminating functions. It becomes a habit for you, and you stop feeling most of your emotions. The feelings are still there, held down by the weight of these things (the clutter). You feel these feelings, but you don't recognize the extent of their destructive effects. Whatever loss you are mourning from the past, it's best to accept that are you feeling some sadness and that the past is not coming back. Let the change happen. Only *you* can let things go. There's freedom and peace of mind when you do that, letting new things in.

She began to cry. I could feel the layers of emotional clutter peeling away. The color was returning to her face. She was breathing more deeply. We went back to tossing. The clutter clothes went to charity. The clothes she currently wore went into the closet and were placed on hangers. Her home was uncovered. There was an incredible peace.

Clothing represents different emotional periods of your life. If you keep a lot of things you don't wear, your clothes closet has become a photo from your past.

Nostalgia rarely helps anyone. It can lessen the pressure of your current difficulties, but it becomes a way to avoid resolving the past. It doesn't help you; rather, it keeps you thinking that the past was better than *right now*. The funny thing is that the moment you are trying to preserve may not have been all that great. In retrospect you can make it look all shiny, but back then you were probably nostalgic about something that had happened even earlier.

EXERCISE

- Move all your clothes to another room. Pretend that you are a buyer for a very important client: you. You don't have much time. You need to quickly go through these clothes and assess whether or not your client would benefit from them or whether they would be a waste of her time. Remember, your client is a powerful person. She wants only what's going to increase the powerful momentum of her life's joy. You were hired because you know her better than anyone.

- Toss the crap with confidence. No one's feelings are hurt. You'd be hurt if you picked the wrong things. That's why you use your surefire, fail-safe discerning eye.

- When you are done, put the keepers in a nice pile and bring them back to the clothes closet and chest of drawers. You've done some great work.

Old Lover Clutter

I worked with a client who, like the diva and her clutter entourage of stuffed animals, also suffered from clutter of the heart. Her clutter, however, was subtler and hidden from view. When I asked this client what she wanted in her life, she replied that she wanted a fantastic boyfriend. She said that she had never had a great relationship, only ones that had ended badly.

Her last relationship had been a long-distance one with a man who lived in Italy. As she told me this, she got a lost look in her eyes. She was in a trance. Her skin lost color. Her voice grew weaker. She was in a virtual-reality trip to a past experience, living in her clutter fantasy world. You couldn't see the clutter on the floor or in closets, but it was in her eyes.

I asked if she had any love letters from him. She said no. So I said, "What about emails?" She took a deep breath and held it. She gritted her teeth. She looked like she was in pain. She said, "Yes." I asked her to show me. She went to her computer and showed me more than five hundred of his emails that she had saved. She was experiencing a lot of emotional pain revisiting them. Her breathing became shallow and jagged. In her sighs, I heard the buildup of tears. All indicators said this was the heart of her clutter.

My client had not been in touch with him for two years. She had no interest in getting back together with him. I said, "It feels pretty bad trying to keep this memory going, doesn't it? It's like someone died, and you won't let them go." She nodded sadly.

There were a few tears. I said, "Let's have a little funeral then. How about deleting the emails?" She took in a quick deep breath and held it. She looked at me for permission. I said, "It's up to you, but if you hang on to this pain, you'll be slowly destroying what is gentle and good in you. It's time to bury the dead. You deserve to have the fullness of life in your heart."

With quiet certainty, she clicked "select all" and hit the delete key.

The emails were gone.

My client took another deep breath. She released it this time. She looked lighter. The dead weight of emotional clutter is debilitating. Shedding that clutter fills you with lightness.

Pointing to her heart, I said, "From now on, you're the caretaker there. You maintain the openness you're feeling. It's not a partner's responsibility. It's yours. You feel good whether or not you are with someone." She nodded knowingly.

EXERCISE

- In your mind, scan over the items in your home. What items from the past have you been keeping that interfere with your present goals?
- Think of a high school football star who is living on the glories of his past and doing nothing

special with his life now. He's hanging on to the memories for the high feelings they give him. How much better would your life be if you had those same feelings about an activity that's a part of your life now? It's doable. It's about letting go of that past "special moment." Think of the things that are waiting to be discovered in your life — things that will come when you let go of your past. You'll never know until you loosen your grip.

- The old items go, and you have an open palm to receive an actual living glory.

The Tyranny of Photos

When helping to clutter bust a client's office, I discovered an epidemic common to other cluttered homes: hundreds of photos not placed in photo albums. I find them piled on shelves and in shoe boxes. Many are in the package sleeves from the developer. I ask my clients when they last looked at the photos, and most of them tell me the day they brought them home from the one-hour photo. They still want to keep them, though. They often tell me they want to put the pictures in a scrapbook, but the years pass and they can't seem to take the necessary action.

The photos are not confined to glossies. Many of my clients have hundreds and sometimes thousands of photos taken with their digital cameras that are now stored on their computers' hard drives. Some clients have had to get an external hard drive to house the digital pics. There are so many stored photos that the clients often confess that they can't find a particular photo they are looking for. Just because these digital photos take up less space by being in a computer rather than filling up drawers and closet space doesn't mean they are not clutter.

Photos are okay, but wouldn't it be great to live with the certainty that there will be countless new good moments to experience? That you will enjoy one great experience after another, every second becoming a snapshot experienced in 3-D with all your senses involved? When you treat something like a treasure, it becomes a treasure. In contrast, when we isolate and designate a few moments as the "good ones," we become rigid and cling to them in our minds, the same way a beggar grips a quarter he finds on the sidewalk. With that old "treasured moment" as the gauge for how you feel about your life, you miss out on what's really going on *now*.

I went through the photos with her, one at a time. I told her to keep the photos that jumped out and animated her heart, that made her feel grateful for the experiences she has had. They are a reaffirmation that she is a deserving person. When we were done, we went to the store and picked out photo albums and colorful magic markers. When we returned, I had her put the photos in the albums. With the markers, she added fun quotes underneath the photos. She even added a special cover that featured a photo of her a' her husband jumping for joy at the Grand Canyon.

When we were done, I had her put the photo albums on the bookshelf with the covers displayed so she could remind herself of her creativity. She had taken old, stagnant memories and used them to create something beautiful. My client was very proud of her work.

I no longer take pictures. I found when I was having a great time and got out the camera to capture the moment, I was suddenly out of the moment. Later, after looking at the photos I took, I found the feeling I got was nothing compared to the actual experience. It was amazingly watered down, a bad duplication. I find it more fulfilling to experience every moment as if it is special. You can actually force it to be less fulfilling by worrying about taking a picture. My friend Diane told me a story about her wedding. She asked the photographer to stop taking photos because she had to keep interrupting what she was doing and posing with people. She told him she was losing out on the fun on the best day of her life, and she didn't care whether she had pictures of her wedding. "I wanted to live it, not pose it."

There are times when photos are comforting and even energizing, for instance, when someone has died. One of my friends told me, "I have one photo of my father in my den. It's very comforting. It makes me feel like he's there with me. I'm not living in the past; I'm honoring his memory. There's a difference. He will always be a part of me, and the part of me he is will always affect my present." Be aware of whether you are holding on to photos to relive the past or to honor a memory.

The Woman Lets Go of the Girl

I was working with a client who was very dissatisfied with her life. She was smart, young, and pretty and seemed to have a lot of potential. But she had no enthusiasm about her life. She exuded sadness.

On the tour of her apartment, I grew curious about her bed. It was a little girl's bed, and it was surrounded with junk: old cardboard boxes, plain plastic storage boxes, piles of clothing that wouldn't fit in her closet and drawers. Her bed seemed like an old castle surrounded by a thick, dull fog.

I began clutter busting right away. Unfortunately, she lost interest after a few minutes. Puzzled, I asked her some questions. She revealed that her mother had dominated her thinking and actions her entire life. Her mother lived on the other side of the country but continued to interfere in her daughter's life.

I asked if she ever spoke up for herself. She told me she was too afraid to say what she felt. I said, "You won't feel free or confident until you make up your own mind and stop depending on your mother. It's caused you to lose your enthusiasm for life. Your mother has convinced you you're still a little girl." When I asked if the bed was the one she slept in as a little girl, she told me it was.

I said, "Parents are heavily invested in their role as caretakers. Sometimes they have a hard time letting go. That's their clutter. By allowing your mother to treat you like a little girl, you've failed to grow up, and both of you are living lies. No one benefits. Your potential for life will not be fulfilled unless you turn it around by deciding that it's your life. You can ignore your mother. You can resent her. Or you can make her see that you can take great care of your life and transition into a different kind of grown-up relationship with her."

I could see the words sink in. I said, "Let's clear this space."

We went through the boxes. They were filled with memorabilia from her childhood. There were many boxes of Barbies and other dolls. There were twenty diaries. There were teen magazines, and she had saved her little-girl clothes. I felt I was in the midst of a prepubescent shrine. I asked her if we could donate everything but the diaries to a charity thrift shop. She agreed.

I knew that the strong language I had used with her had sunk in when she decided to throw out the diaries without even looking at them. Her doubt and dependence evaporated. She looked and felt like an adult. Her voice was stronger.

We agreed that it was time to let go of the bed. We removed the boxes and then dismantled the bed and took it out of the room. When we returned to the room, we stood in the empty space.

I said, "This is the next stage of your life. It belongs to you. This is the source of everything you will do from now on."

I brought her nostalgia collection to a charity. When I called my client the next day, she told me she had purchased a bed right after I left; she had asked for same-day delivery. It was a queen-size bed. I told her that was fitting for someone like her. When I asked how she had slept, she told me that normally she wakes up tired, but that morning she had woken up feeling well rested.

EXERCISE

- Pretend you are a reporter for a newspaper and that you are assigned to do a feature story about yourself. But you will not be interviewing yourself. Rather, you will base your life story on what you see in your home.
- Deduce the story from what you see and feel. Be objective. Expose the truth. Write it down.
- Read what you wrote. Let it affect you. Great changes come when the truth is told.

Burying the Dead

I was hired by an eighty-two-year-old architect and artist. He couldn't seem to get anything done in his office, and he wanted me to help him clear out the clutter. I was more drawn to the guest room next to the office. This room felt heavy and dark, even with the lights on and the sun streaming through the window. Someone who believed in ghosts might say the room felt possessed.

In the room was a sofa bed that wouldn't close. Around

the sofa were many cardboard boxes filled with papers. These boxes were filled with nostalgia items. Most of them related to his wife, who had died five years earlier. She was an opera star. He hadn't touched or looked at any of these papers since she died. Everything was covered in layers of dust. It felt like she was buried there.

We went through the old photos, and it was clear that he loved looking at the photos of his wife. He reminisced with each picture. After he finished looking at each one, he tossed it into the trash. I realized he was saying good-bye to his wife. He had never really done that. He handled all her knickknacks, figurines, 78 records, and postcards, and then let them go. It took about three hours to go through all her belongings.

When we were done, he looked like a man freed of a heavy burden. His heart soared. He revealed to me that he was now thinking of getting remarried and felt very open to finding a girlfriend.

The room felt lighter. I tried the sofa bed again. This time it closed.

You Can't Take It with You

Like many people, you most likely expend a lot of energy holding on to your past. But eventually you'll die. When you're not here anymore, your stuff won't mean anything to you. It won't mean much to anyone else either. Your things are not *you*. They are your memories, your ghosts.

Here is a case in point. I was hired by a woman to clutter bust her recently deceased mother's apartment. When I got there, the lady and her two sisters and brother were combing through their dead mom's stuff, looking for goodies. Their mother was a photographer. She collected cameras from the 1940s up to the present day. Her husband had died ten years ago, and she had saved his camera.

Lying around the apartment were the mother's postcards from her travels around the world, thousands of photos she had taken over her lifetime, piles of random papers and newspaper clippings, old coins, her grade school and high school memorabilia, and books on almost every country in the world. And there were her personal diaries. The apartment was a time capsule of this woman's life.

It was like a mausoleum. It felt heavy and cold. It felt like their mother's stuff had died with her. Nothing in the space felt alive.

The children wanted nothing to do with their mother's personal items. Instead they had a screaming fight over her home entertainment center: the big-screen TV, the DVD player, the stereo receiver, and the DVD and CD collection. This fighting was the manifestation of clutter from the family's relationships. I asked them to be quiet. I told them it was time for another funeral. I placed an empty chair in the middle of the room. I said, "Imagine your mother has decided to visit you one last time before she goes, and she's sitting in this chair."

The children became quieter.

I said, "She's aware of all the papers and the books and the cameras and even the TV stuff. She doesn't care about any of that crap. She has no need for it. What she really sees is the only thing that mattered in her life. She sees you. She feels good about who you've become. She's excited about your lives. She wants you to enjoy each other. She said you can keep what you want, or you can toss it all. She doesn't care. She's just glad she got one more chance to see her family."

There were some tears. The anger was gone. So were the bitterness and neediness. There was lightness in the room.

The son said he wanted one of the mother's journals. He wanted to know more about what she had felt. He said to his mom, "I promise I'll toss it out when I'm done." That brought some big laughs.

One of the daughters took a photo that her mom had taken of the mountains and the ocean. She told her mom it reminded her of her.

After that, the children were practically begging each other to take the home entertainment stuff. The rest of their mother's things ended up in the dumpster.

What's essential to you? What satisfies you? What do you think you need, and what really matters? What comes to your heart when you think about these things?

EXERCISE

- Imagine you've died and that you're floating above your home. Suddenly the door to your place is open, and a hundred strangers file in.

Watch them sort through all your belongings: your clothes, your electronics, the files on your computer, your shoes, your kitchen items, your books, your CDs, everything in your files and on your desk, your jewelry, your furniture, your garage, and everything in your closets and drawers.

- Listen to their reactions to your stuff. See what is left behind after they leave. See the garbage men come and take and toss the leftovers. See new people move in and distribute their clutter.

The attachment to your stuff is in your mind. When you use your mind to discern what is really important, you break your attachments to the past, and you let go of your clutter.

Chapter Four

CLUTTER REPRESENTS
FEAR OF CHANGE

Change, which has the force of the universe behind it, is constant. Nothing is stable or permanent, yet we have a deep-seated, unconscious fear of change. When that fear comes into our lives, we often become rigid and unhappy. We find ourselves grabbing on to anything that gives us a false comfort of stability, even though it belies true happiness. Our obsession and worry about the future is clutter. It's often based on our fear of death, our own loss of permanence. If we have a lot of things, we sometimes support a false belief of eternal being and invincibility.

Often we manifest clutter to resist change. Resistance gives you a feeling of pressure, and pressure gives you definition. The definitions are your problems. They give you a false sense of identity. People learn to assess their lives, who they are, through their difficulties. It's how we are brought up. Now is the time to drop identifying labels, to experience life as it comes. And life changes every second.

Allow things to come and go. This will bring the very happiness that you were hoping your things would bring you.

The Physiology of Clutter

If you hang on to things, you will *feel* as if your life is staying the same. Clutter gives the illusion of stability. But then your life becomes a nostalgia act. It may not seem that way to you, but it's true. People try to mummify the past to maintain a mental homeostasis. However, this causes life to take on rigor mortis. You lose flexibility. You're slowly becoming embalmed without realizing it. Suddenly a big change comes, and it's difficult to adapt. Resistance takes over. You refuse to acknowledge what is happening. Anger, defensiveness, and denial rise to the occasion.

After 9/11, people described the events as if they were a dream. There was a refusal to accept the events because it meant change on a very deep level. Some people still won't accept what happened.

Our existence is an ocean. The waves of activity affect and move everything. Movement is change. Nothing is solid; nothing can remain the same. The solid forms you see everywhere are made up of atoms. Electrons spin around the nucleus at speeds of billions of revolutions per second. They do not repeat the same spin patterns. They are not predictable. Anything is possible. Everything in life is made up of atoms. Thus, stability is an impossibility, even on the tiniest scale. Change is inevitable.

Anything can happen. Accepting this provides peace of

mind. This is the only stability we can have: to know that change is our nature, the nature of everything. Your acceptance of this subtle truth settles the heart and mind. When you are clutter busting, you accept that some of your possessions are no longer part of your ever-changing life. You move with the discovery. You are moving with the universe, rather than fighting the powerful force of change.

At one point, people had to accept that the earth was not flat. I'm certain they had a hard time when they first saw a globe! Many people died still fearing they'd fall off the edge of the world. People tend to stay mired in an image of the past, even though it no longer reflects what is actually happening. They resist accepting that change has happened — is happening — and they keep the things that remind them of how they want to keep seeing things, even though it is not a true reflection of what is.

Resistance to clutter busting is a belief in the illusion of stability. How much longer can you believe in this "flat earth"?

You have control over your choices. The problem is, most choices are based on habit. These habits are often a source of problems. When you honestly look at what is happening in your life right now, you begin to break a habit. I'm encouraging you to look. You don't have to leave your home to do this. It is right here in front of you, waiting. Change is like a dog that is utterly enthusiastic to see you the moment you decide to greet it. There is no right time to begin other than now.

Clutter Busting the "Kid"

Becoming an adult, leaving behind the world of being a child and a teenager, is a powerful point of change in people's lives. The momentum of this change propels people into their professional and personal lives. Yet many have not fully made this transition. I've seen a lot of adults hiding things as if their parents will show up any moment and find these things and punish them. It seems as though they never got a real send-off when they ventured out on their own. Deep down, some parents don't want to let their children go because they identify with the job of keeping them alive. It can be easy for some adults to remain as a kid in their heads because they don't have to make choices, but to live that way is a fantasy.

I worked with a client who wanted me to organize her home office. When I got there, she complained about her son's office, which was right next to hers. He was twenty-eight years old and still living at home. Her office was clean. His looked as though a hurricane had gone through it. She kept asking him to clean it up, and he kept refusing. She'd end up helping him clean it, and then he would mess it up again.

I told her she needed to kick him out of the nest. He needed to get his own office — outside her house. He was clearly addicted to having Mommy take care of him. He needed to learn to take care of himself and be self-sufficient, and he would not change until she told him to go. She was in some way cherishing the role of being Mommy and felt guilty about booting out her baby. She now understood the need to stop living in the past and gave her son a month to move out.

Becoming Her Own Doctor

Sometimes clients have very strong beliefs about themselves that are detrimental. Even though these beliefs don't serve them, they will resist change, defending the beliefs and continuing to surround themselves with the supportive evidence — their clutter. They will resist anything that threatens the invested idea they have of themselves. I am thinking of one client in particular, who was a recluse. She was very pale and hunched over, and she spoke incessantly. She was constantly worried. My client was also obsessed with medical books. She had more than three hundred volumes. She had a book for almost every possible illness.

When I asked her if she read them, she said she had read only part of a few of them. She told me she didn't like to read. Then when I asked her if she would ever read all those books, she looked overwhelmed. Weakened. She couldn't answer. This meant the books were clutter. I said, "Good, we can toss them out." She got very flustered and refused. I said, "You hate to read, you've had these books for years, they will remain in these boxes for years to come. You will never read them."

She explained to me that she had a lot of medical problems and that the books helped her understand them. I asked her if she had all the diseases in the books. She said no, but the books were there in the event that she acquired the diseases.

I asked, "What if you never get those diseases?" She didn't want to talk about that. I said, "You've admitted to me that you won't read these books, so if you keep them, they won't be of help." She didn't say anything.

I asked her what she wanted. She said, "I don't want to be sick anymore. I'm tired of being in pain."

I replied, "I'm not interested in what you don't want. Tell me what you *want*."

She said with great strength and conviction, "I want to be healthy." She looked clear and calm for the first time. She sat up straight. Color came into her face. She looked healthy. I said to her, "You've transformed. How are you feeling?" She looked surprised. She said, "I don't feel any pain." She was amazed. It had been years since she had been pain free. I said, "This shows how powerful a person you are. You used to identify yourself as weak and sickly. You kept the books to remind yourself of that condition. But you couldn't read the books because deep down you knew it wasn't true. So can we let go of the books now?"

Amazingly, she still wanted to keep them. This indicated that she had some deeper emotional attachment to them. I said, "If you're not going to read the books and you just showed yourself that you can make yourself healthy, why do you need the books?"

She said that according to a lot of people, the books were supposed to be really good. I replied, "You're talking about someone else's opinion of them, not yours. I'm only interested in how you feel about them." No one had ever said that to her before.

She had surrounded herself for years with people who told her what to do. These people were clutter because they were getting in the way of her enjoying her life. The clutter was blocking her intuition. The moment was powerful. I could see she knew she could take care of herself. She became frightened and wanted to go back to the clutter.

I asked, "Do you want to remain sick, because that is what will happen if you keep warehousing these books and putting your faith in other people's hands." She couldn't answer.

It was as if all the people she'd placed above her as experts were waiting for her to answer. She unconsciously felt they would be angry if she let them go. She was keeping this clutter alive by depending on it.

She said, "I want to feel good! I want to make my own decisions. I'm tired of people telling me what to do!"

I asked, "What do you want instead?"

She answered, "I want to take good care of myself. I know how to do that better than anybody else!" She glowed and looked amazingly powerful. There was no trace of illness in her body, voice, or face. She had let go of the clutter in her heart and mind.

I said, "Let's go through the books." We let go of about 95 percent of them. She agreed to donate them to the local library. She kept a few books on intuitive self-healing.

When you go through your own clutter, question everything, especially the things that scare you, because those are the things to let go of. You'll learn a lot about yourself, and it will become clear what you really care about.

- Take out some paper and cut it into small strips. Write on each piece something that you feel is wrong with you or your life. This can be anything from how you feel negative about yourself, to how you think you look, how you believe others see you, or how you think you should be. "I'm dumb." "I wish I was pretty." "I'm fat." "People hate me." "I wish I was better at _____."

- Place all the pieces of paper on the floor so you can read them all as you stand looking over them.

- Take a good look. They are misconceptions about your life. Your mind has created these hurdles, and they don't help you. They are clutter. You are a fluid presence. You are pure awareness of your experiences. What you wrote on the paper is insignificant and not worth your time.

- Gather up the papers. Tear the clutter up and throw it in the recycling. It's time for you to grow past wrong assessments of yourself. I believed in you enough to write this book. Now's a great time for you to go with the momentum of change.

Millennium Lady

My client lived on the second floor of a dilapidated guesthouse in Long Beach. I entered through the kitchen, where I was greeted by huge dust-covered spiderwebs. They stretched from the floor halfway up the walls. Large spiders walked casually over them. The image was right out of the dungeon in *Frankenstein*.

I asked, "What's up with the spiderwebs?" She indicated she had spoken with a psychic who told her that spiderwebs were good. "They trap the negative energies." I asked her, "How do you feel about them?" She gave me an odd look. She wasn't used to hearing a question like that — even from herself. She surprised herself by saying, "I don't like them." I told her that was reason enough to let them go. She agreed, so I got some paper towels and wiped them away.

This woman was in her fifties. But when she spoke she sounded like a five-year-old girl, and a whiny one at that. She was living with strong inner clutter. When you unconsciously think you're five, you have no responsibilities. You think other people will take care of you, even though they won't. I knew her life was very much about resistance.

She had a dog with a bad leg who was afraid of men. The dog was tiny and kept looking at me with horrified eyes as if I would recognize it was clutter and toss it out. It also feared that the clutter would topple over on it and kill it. This was a reflection of the woman's feelings. Animals feel our clutter and sometimes internalize it themselves.

The next amazing clutter item was a tremendous amount of packaged food stacked high on a towering shelf. The woman had purchased it in 1999 for the feared impending millennium disaster. It was now long past "doomsday." Some of this food had exploded right out of its packaging. That usually happens a year after the expiration date. Some of the boxes had been nibbled through by rodents and were leaking their contents. Some of the plastic containers containing liquids were bulging. I figured since this was her fear manifested, the same kind of scenario was going on in her body: bloating, ulcers, constipation.

Even though nothing happened at the turn of the century, she felt certain that she needed to keep the rancid rations. But while she talked about them, she rubbed her head, and looked off, and her breathing was short. She spoke quickly, in a high-pitched voice. She was in a major clutter trance. I felt she was holding on to this crap because she had bought the rations in a panicked state of mind. Since she was a fearful woman, she felt there was always a disaster imminent. She reckoned it was good to hang on to the rations. This was a reaffirmation that the world is a dangerous place and she should beware!

When I said, "Everything is okay now; you can let these things go," she told me to shut up. I was speaking to her core clutter. She believed that the world was a very dark and scary place that would eventually eat her alive. I told her, "If you tell me to shut up again, I'll go and leave you standing in this mess for the rest of your life."

This snapped her back to the moment, and she apologized. The glaze in her eyes was gone. She took in the nasty state of her kitchen. She said, "I can't believe I let myself live like this. Okay, I'll let it go."

I took down all the millennium food and put it in three gigantic trash bags.

As I was taking it outside to the trash cans, she asked me if I wanted any of the food.

This was the last vestige of her clutter talking. I said, "Are you kidding me?" She laughed. More inner clutter went.

Next I moved onto the roof outside her kitchen window. There was an exercise bike sitting on the edge of the roof looking out over the backyard. Cobwebs extended from the bike to the roof. The bike was covered with rust. I asked her when she had last ridden it. She said she never rode the bike, but she wanted to. I asked her how long she had owned the bike. She told me five years.

If someone owns something and they put it in a difficult place to reach and the thing begins to fall apart, the thing is clutter. She was keeping the bike to make her feel guilty as a way to get her to exercise. But, as you can see, guilt does not work. It is simply self-cruelty. It prevents change. The person gets to keep whipping herself with bad feelings.

When I asked if we could let the bike go, she told me she wanted to keep it. I asked her if she was ever going to ride the bike, and she whined, "I don't know."

I said, "Five years is a long time not to know. Maybe

this could be one less thing in your life to think about. Hey, the bike is facing away from the house. It wants to fly off the roof. How about we let it go?"

She raised her foot and with tremendous vitality kicked it off the roof. When the bike hit the ground, it shattered.

I said, "Finally you got some exercise out of the thing." She laughed.

It is an amazing thing when people take back their lives.

EXERCISE

- What do you own that signifies fear about an event that has never happened? To hang on to that thing disrupts the peace in your home. It doesn't matter whether or not you can see it. It gives off an alarm. It keeps you on edge. Imagine how much tension that adds up to over months and years. Stand in the middle of your home with your eyes closed, and see if you can spot the item with your heart.

- Are you living with superstitions? These can be anything that you own that someone told you will protect you from bad events. Believing that there are evil things out there that want to destroy you is clutter. You get what you believe. This kind of thinking is not helping you. Letting these things go opens you to the belief that you live in a loving, helpful universe.

- What things do you own that want to leave your home? Take a look and see what is waving its hand at you. Sometimes just the way things are placed makes it obvious. I worked with a couple that had placed a pretty high pile of stuff in the hallway right next to their *front* door. It was as if the stuff was ready to walk right out of the house. They let the things go.

A Son's Clutter Never Left Home

Remember my client from earlier in the chapter who needed to kick her son out of this nest? Here is another example of parents struggling with accepting that their role as parents has changed. The couple hired me telling me that I could look in any room in the house except for one. I said, "That's the room we're clutter busting." They replied, "You can't; it's a mess."

I said, "That's why I'm here."

When I opened the door to the room, I saw that the entire floor was piled five feet high with clutter. It was impossible to tell what was underneath the junk because it was covered with big white sheets of broken Styrofoam. They wanted to hide the mess. This put a frame around the heap of disorder.

They were embarrassed. The husband said, "This is

our son's room." It turned out the son had moved out a year ago, to a place about a mile away. I immediately took away the Styrofoam to see what I was dealing with. There were sports jerseys and trophies, comic books, old videotapes, old worn clothing and shoes, sports posters, books, and other stuff their son had used as a kid. If they had wanted to make the room into a museum of their son's life, they would have had all the ingredients.

I asked, "Is your son coming back for any of this?" The father answered, "He's got his own stuff." He didn't want to say "no" because he didn't want to admit his son had really moved out. Part of this was him subconsciously leaving the door open in case the son wanted to return.

When I suggested that we toss it out, it was clear that it hadn't occurred to them that they could. The mother said, "I guess."

I told them, "If your son wanted any of this stuff, he would have taken it with him. This stuff is still here because the two of you are hanging on to your jobs as parents. It can be hard to let go of the job in your mind because you did it for eighteen years. There's a lot of momentum behind something like that. You must have done a great job because he only moved a mile away. He must like you."

The mother smiled and said, "Yes, he visits us once a week."

I said, "Letting go of that responsibility frees you up to do something new with your lives. Plus, it allows your son to become independent, a man. You want that for him, don't you?" They both agreed, and we immediately began the tossing. They went at it with a vengeance. Before I even finished a question about whether I could toss a thing, they were saying, "Just toss it."

The mother found a bunch of art supplies mixed in with her son's junk. She told me she'd always wanted to do artwork, but she never had time.

I said, "Here's something new coming into your life. You can create as much art as you'd like now." She was glowing. There were alternatives to being a parent they hadn't considered, having been parents for so long. They were attaining a new sense of freedom.

The father talked about how he would like to turn the room into his office. He was excitedly telling me and his wife what he would like to put on the walls and where he would put the desk.

Within a few hours, we reached a much-stained carpet. The father was so inspired to keep moving forward that he began to tear up the carpet, creating a dust storm. The woman started coughing, so she went to their bedroom and began tossing her own old clothing from the closet.

They didn't need me anymore. I wished them well and left them to their brand-new life.

Chapter Five

CLUTTER IS AN ADDICTION

As we have seen clearly by now, many of us have the mistaken notion that our things are sacred and we are not. Because of that belief we use the clutter in our life to try to make ourselves feel more powerful. This backfires because we find ourselves still feeling weak and miserable, and we remain stuck in the past. Because this process exhausts us, we don't have the clarity to see what we are doing. We try to protect ourselves by resisting change and acquiring more things. We are junkies to clutter. We use things to keep away pain. We use our stuff to manipulate a feeling of joy. We care more about the feeling we associate with a thing than about the thing itself; we crave the feeling we associate with the thing. Clutter is an addiction because we feel uncomfortable when we don't have the feeling anymore.

Are you like this? You think you want an item, but unconsciously you crave the feeling associated with it. You need the "hit" the feeling gives you. You mistakenly think that the thing contains happiness, joy, and passion. The thing does not have life; it's an inert object. Realizing this, and the mechanics of your relationship with this stuff you are addicted to, will give you the distance to stop operating in an endlessly destructive cycle. This stuff loses its hold. Clarity and peace of mind take over.

Self-Insulation

Clutter keeps you from feeling. It acts as an emotional insulator in the same way that drugs and booze do. Like a drink, it wears off, and then you have to acquire more to be numb. Clutter buries you alive.

People defend their clutter, sometimes even when they see that it no longer serves them. This happens because they are looking at the thing and not at the feeling *behind* the thing. When you decide to keep something, you are keeping the feeling you link with it. If it is a powerful feeling, you may not want to let go of what you are experiencing: the high. You crave that sensation.

Our lives can be pretty dull and repetitious. So when we experience a strong sensation from a particular object, we don't want to lose the buzz. But as with all highs, the buzz doesn't last long. The body adapts to any experience, and the experience becomes normal. That is when your craving for that feeling comes in. You want that sensation back. You need a hit. So you go and buy something else. You add another thing to your life. You are giving yourself a fix and adding more junk as a result. There's no end to this madness. All the shifting from great highs to deep lows wears you down.

You can continue the pattern. Or you can stop. Right now.

Time to Peel

This insulation you surround yourself with is a lie. You *seem* to feel better. But the sadness and fear and anger are still eating away at you. You are just not feeling the effects, since these feelings are temporarily covered up.

It is pretty rare for us to be completely honest with ourselves. We have been taught to say that "everything is fine" so that people think we have it together. We pretend we are happy. You can also put an end to this dynamic. You have enough. Much more than enough. It is time to edit down to the essentials. Peel away the layers of insulation and see that under all the clutter is your happiness, patiently waiting, smiling back at you.

When you clear out the excess in your life, the naturally spontaneous things that make a difference in your life begin to appear. They enter quietly. They don't take up space. They illuminate your life and show your brilliance. This brings in self-gratitude, which is basically fulfillment manifested. You love your life. Nothing needs to be added. No additives, no preservatives — naturally sweetened.

Each layer gone brings renewal. This is the same feeling you thought the clutter would give you, only it's sustainable. You lose your desire for insulation because you see that it keeps you from feeling this joy.

How could you be happier than that?

The Nature of Attachment

Imagine this scenario. You hear a song on the radio, and it sends you soaring emotionally. When the song is over, you want to own a copy of it, and you go and buy the CD online or an MP3 file on iTunes. It's not the song you want, though; it's the *feeling* you got while listening to the song. The desire to have that feeling again is your motivation behind the purchase. If you knew you could get that feeling from a tomato, you'd go to the produce section of your local grocery store.

Joy is a great thing. The only problem is that nothing is consistent. There's no certainty that the object will ever reproduce that joy again. The high wears off. If you listen to the song fifteen times in a row, it will start to become an irritation. But your mind keeps the memory of that original joy and its source burned into your awareness. "This is where I found happiness. It's rare. I must hang on to it."

You wind up feeling disappointed, though, since the objects no longer give you that original joy. That's too hard to face, so you suppress the feeling. You bury the items in a closet, a drawer, the garage, or under the bed.

As you begin this process, admit to yourself that most of the things you own aren't going to make you happy. Having so much clutter only causes you pain and confusion. In the end, you keep the essentials — the things that matter right now.

EXERCISE

- Take out all your CDs and cassettes and albums from their storage containers and place them in the middle of the room. If your music is in MP3s in your computer, take a look at the list of songs on your computer screen. With each one, ask yourself if you would purchase and listen to this recording today. You may be surprised at your answer. Again, the first answer is always the truthful one. If you are unsure, play the song and see how it makes you feel. Do you want that feeling in your life?

Clutterers Anonymous

I was sitting in a client's extremely cluttered living room. She had to pull stuff off the couch just so I could sit down. She told me that she and her husband are chronic clutterers. They go to Clutterers Anonymous, a 12-step program for people who admit they are addicted to clutter.

Sitting in the midst of her excessive junk, she revealed the beginnings of her clutter history. The week before her birth, seven of her relatives died. She said, "I was born into a dying world. By holding on to stuff, I will ensure that I live forever."

I said, "After you die, your clutter will still be here. Someone is going to come in here and be really unhappy about having to clear out all your stuff. Your clutter will outlive you. I think you are feeling guilty because you lived. How about if you reverse your viewpoint and be grateful that you are alive? Gratitude erases guilt."

She said she understood and then continued to detail her behavior. She was caught up in her addiction. She told me that she couldn't drive past anything sitting out on a curb or alleyway without stopping to pick it up and put it in her car. She said she would do this whether or not she needed the item; it was compulsive. Once the item was in her possession, she explained, she didn't care about it anymore. She would bring it home and put it anywhere in her house. That is why her home was a junkyard.

I asked her, "How does it feel when you see something sitting out on the curb?"

She said, "I get an intense buzz. I'm really excited. I can't get the thing fast enough. It doesn't make any sense. I can't help myself. I have to have it."

When I asked her how she feels after getting the thing in her truck and driving home, she admitted, "I feel let down, and guilty. I'm very ashamed. I hope no one saw me."

I told her, "You go for this thing because of the *feeling* you get. Afterward the feeling is gone, and you feel empty."

My client made a great discovery. These were the symptoms of a drug addict. She was getting a fix when she picked up junk on the side of the road. When you use things to make yourself feel better, you don't care about the thing; you just want the high you'll get from it. You push away the memories of how you'll feel afterward and think only about the high itself.

She said, "Yes, I just want that feeling."

I told her, "All this crap in your house represents the used needles and empty drug vials of your roadside clutter drug encounter." She had never had to be this honest about her situation. I told her to close her eyes.

I said, "Imagine you're driving down the road. Suddenly on the side of the road you see an old dining room chair. How does it make you feel?"

She said, "My heart is beating very fast. I'm excited. I'm sweating. I want to pull over and get it."

I instructed her, "I want you to skip ahead and tell me how it feels driving home with the chair in the back of your truck?"

She said, "I'm feeling very nauseated. I hate that I did it. I don't know why I can't stop."

"I want you to look in the rearview mirror and see the chair, and double what you are feeling. These are the feelings these things really give you."

When you're addicted to something, you see only the brief high, the feeling that lasts a few seconds. You shut out the real feelings, the significant ones that are telling the truth, the ones that will last until you get the high again. The high lasts a few seconds and then back to these feelings of sadness and anger and despair.

I said to her, "The clutter makes you feel wretched. You are living with other people's trash. You can stop this habit by remembering the real effect of picking up other people's junk. If you feel the desire to pull over, remember what it feels like a minute after you have it in your car, and how you feel when you have to carry it into your home, hoping no one sees you, and having to live in a home that feels like a garbage dump. Imagine you are driving down the road and you see an old lamp sitting out on the curb. How do you feel?"

She said, "I want it, but I know it's going to make me feel like shit. I don't know what to do."

"Imagine you are driving down the road. You pull into your driveway. There is nothing in the car. You walk proudly into your home, carrying nothing. Your home is clean and peaceful. How do you feel?"

She said, "Oh, my God, I feel free! This is great. I love it!"

"You are driving down the road; there is an old TV sitting on the curb. What..."

She said, "I drive right past it."

I told her to open her eyes. She looked relieved.

"Let's start tossing things," she said joyfully.

The tossing began. She was on a mission. She let go of a tremendous amount of items. We took seven trips worth of the stuff in her truck to the local charity.

EXERCISE

- Find an unused item in your house that you're having trouble tossing. At one time you had to have this item. But here it is, in your home, serving no purpose. It's not making your life any better; it is actually causing you pain. But you can't let it go. That's an addiction. You bought or acquired the thing so you would feel good. You are letting an inanimate object take advantage of you.

• Now imagine that the item is gone, as if it was never there. How does that feel? Be very honest. Is there a sense of freedom?

Often when my clients let go of an object, a week later they can't even remember what the thing was.

EXERCISE

• Imagine that you have died. Your stuff is still in your home. Pretend that you are the new person moving into the space. Sort through the stuff and remove the things you have no interest in. Keep the things you like, but put them in a place that would better suit you.

• Now imagine you have died but that you're not totally gone because you're a ghost. No one knows you're dead yet. But they're going to find out very soon, and they'll be coming to your home and going through your things. Find the insignificant junk that you've been hanging on to for years and toss it out before everyone discovers it.

Hey, you're still alive. There are still a lot of things you can do with your life. Now is the time to do them. You bought this book. You must care a lot about yourself.

What else do you want to do now to show how much more you care?

Spiritual Addiction

Spirituality can also be an addiction. You crave enlightenment. You may be unhappy that you don't have it. You may be chasing an image and concept of complete happiness and bliss. This is the same as craving some item, hoping it will make you feel happier. Maybe you read or heard about it and knew you had to have it. Your life would continue to suck until you acquired this "precious thing." Maybe you go from teacher to guru to seminar to self-help books.

Many of my clients have an overload of self-help books and pictures of their teachers placed higher than their own photos and those of their loved ones. Essentially, they are unhappy and are chasing an elusive goal of *eternal happiness*. The more they chase it, the further away from happiness they get. They have become spiritual junkies.

Different gurus pitch their version of happiness. Reincarnation, Tantric sex, rebirthing, astrology, and so on. Choose your drug and get your fix. None of them sets you free permanently. They give a temporary buzz. And then you want the feeling back. A craving has developed, an addiction. You feel lousy. You think you will feel better only when you get the "special buzz" back.

One of my female clients had a lot of spiritual books. She'd read them all and didn't want to reread them, but she didn't want to let them go. She told me if she got rid of them she feared she would forget all that she'd learned.

I asked, "Do you still remember the alphabet?"

She was puzzled but said, "Yes."

I said, "You remember what you need to know when you need to know it."

She asked, "I will remember on a need-to-know basis?" I nodded.

She let the books go.

Know that no thing and no one is going to heal you. Some people cling to the idea of a spiritual path, or a guru, because they fail to realize that the power to be happy resides within them. They must believe in something because they have little belief in themselves. When you stop chasing, you get what you unknowingly crave: simple peace. Nothing elaborate — just peace.

What is the carrot that keeps leading you into a life without real fulfillment?

"To Do" Piles

A great way to cure yourself of your clutter addiction is to tackle your "to do" piles. A client hired me to clutter bust his home, and the first thing I noticed was his dining room table, stacked two feet high with papers. Many had spilled off the table and were scattered about the floor. I asked about their significance.

He told me it was his "to do" table. These were the things he told himself that he wanted and needed to take care of. The pile was a shuffled heap. There was no order to this mess. I asked him if this system worked. Looking embarrassed, he told me, "No."

I sensed he felt an obligation to the papers. They were other people's priorities. He told me it had been like this for years. He kept telling himself he would get through the stack. A lot of my clients have "to do" piles. I am immediately suspicious about them. I told him this pile was a sinkhole in his life. The clutter kept him fixated on and overwhelmed about the future. It prevented him from living right now and being happy.

When I dug into the pile, I found that many of the papers were from self-help seminars that other people wanted him to attend. There were many articles he was "supposed" to read. There were letters from people wanting him to buy a product or service. I asked him quickly if these were things *he* actually wanted to do. He had never asked himself that before. He kept saying no, timidly at first, and with strength and assurance as the momentum grew.

Very soon he delved into the papers and began quickly tossing them into the big clutter recycling bag. We were done in an hour. The table was clear for the first time in years. My client was amazed and enlivened. He had done all the work — I had just gotten him rolling in the right direction, just as I'm doing for you right now.

EXERCISE

- Find your "to do" pile and begin to go through the items with an ultimatum attitude: Nothing waits until tomorrow. Clean it all up today. If you're hesitating about something, you either think the decision is difficult and you procrastinate, which only increases the pain, or you do not want to do it. Be honest with yourself. Piles of undone things are like dirty laundry: their smell will extend through the entire house and foul up your life. It is okay to pass up "opportunities" that do not interest you. Sometimes people will avoid letting something go because they feel there will not be another opportunity. But if it does not feel right, it is *not for you*. Let it go, and be open to new changes. You will know when and if something is for you. When you get into the habit of letting something go right away, you are thriving on freedom. It feels great to say, "No, thanks."

Getting into the habit of completing things is another great sensation. You are a prisoner of a task if you start and stop it midstream. You may not look at the undone work, hoping to keep it out of your awareness. But it is like the hungry baby birds constantly chirping for food. The influence will be felt and throw you off.

When I first meet most of my clients, they have stacks of unfinished projects. They get used to living that way and no longer consciously notice the effect. But it is there. Your life is probably constipated in this way. This ultimatum is the way out. Finish things now.

Chapter Six

CLEARING CLUTTER TO MAKE ROOM FOR CLARITY

Many of us live with very little clarity. We may think we see things as they are, but our visions are fear based and coated with illusion. This viscous coating makes it extremely difficult to see things as they are. Your actions may be soaked in the fear of loss. This is motivated by the deep-seated fear of death. The *idea* of your life is another "thing." You may react to your fears by acquiring things to give you the *sense* of permanence, which further clouds your vision. It makes you stumble over things you don't see, and you become even more fearful.

By peeling away the extraneous layers of clutter, you gain clarity. The fewer things you cling to, the greater the value of your life *now*. By letting go of the things in your home, you look at your entire life. You see what is unnecessary in the way you live, in the people you associate with, in the ways you spend your time, in your beliefs.

You intuitively begin to declutter the rest of your life.

In the Bedroom

A woman hired me to help clutter bust her home. Since her husband was at work, she felt comfortable letting me know that though they'd been married for twenty-five years, their endless fighting was causing them to consider divorce. I immediately said, "Let's check out the bedroom." A couple's bedroom reveals the health of the relationship. It's the communications center. As I suspected, their bedroom was a great mess.

The first thing I noticed was an immense TV perched precariously on their clothes dresser. It looked like a gargoyle that watched them while they slept. TV takes you to another place. It eliminates your need to have conversation. If it's in your bedroom, it separates you from your partner. Lying in bed, a healthy couple can talk intimately. They can make love. But a TV takes away your need for connection. We agreed to take the TV out of the room. But then she admitted she was frightened by how her husband might react and she made me bring it back into the room.

She saw it sitting back on the dresser and didn't look happy. I asked her why she wanted it there. She was used to her husband being the decision maker, and she didn't want to rock the boat. They weren't talking because she was afraid to be honest with him.

This is an example of how clutter can be an obstruction between two people. Emotions are suppressed and projected onto the item, which turns it into a barrier.

I felt she was reacting to her husband as she probably

reacted to her father when she was growing up. She was transferring the feelings from the past into the present. It's common to discover unresolved associated qualities when you go through your clutter. When I asked her about her relationship with her father, she blanched and was silent, as though swallowing the words she wanted to say. She finally told me that she was constantly afraid to tell her father what she was thinking and that she never opposed him.

I told my client that her husband was not her father, that she was now a grown woman who could make up her own mind. She had trouble realizing this, so I led her through a visual separation. I told her to close her eyes and imagine her father. Next, I instructed her to imagine her father layered upon her husband. I had her see the two of them moving in sync. I said this was the source of her problems. I then directed her to separate them. Following my instructions, she put her father on the moon and her husband in her bed next to her at night. I said, "This is how things are. It's best to keep them that way. It simplifies your life." She smiled.

She asked me to take the TV back out of the bedroom.

EXERCISE

- Sit silently on the floor of your bedroom. Spend a little time taking in your room. Get a sense of what fits. What feels right being there? What supports your rest and peace of mind?

- Now sense what creates discord or unrest. What feels out of place? What's in your bedroom that makes you feel agitated? These are the things that must leave your bedroom. Remove them now.
- Come back to your bedroom. Sit again. Feel the difference.
- Take another scan of the room. What else can you let go of?

Under the Bed

Let's continue with my client's story. The next step I took was to look under the couple's bed. The space was jampacked. There was no room for even one more thing.

Your bed needs to be a place of peace. It's where intimacy is generated and maintained. Anything that blocks that intimacy is clutter. I told her, "The things under your bed resonate energy. You don't see the items, but you feel them. If you cook lasagna in the kitchen, you smell it in the living room. If you've got something that you don't want to deal with and you try hiding it under the bed, it's hidden visually but it's still calling out to you. You may as well put it all under the covers with you."

This bed situation applies to single people too. Most people have clutter under their beds. This kind of storage hinders you because it disturbs the one place you should be able to count on to find peace and quiet. This mess can manifest into a general sense of agitation or a difficulty falling asleep or, more troubling, the feeling that you didn't get enough sleep, even though you had eight or nine hours.

There was so much clutter under the couple's bed that it was difficult to pull it apart. It felt as though I was sticking my hand into a clogged drain. I finally retrieved a ski jacket, which was followed by an unmarked box and then a big clear plastic storage container filled with financial papers. In the end, there were more than twenty items. I piled them in front of her bed. If I hadn't pulled them out myself, I wouldn't have believed you could put that much stuff under the bed — the magician's old hat trick!

She looked like a dog that had just been shown the business it had done on the living room rug. But rather than push her nose in it, I asked her to get down on the floor and take a look at the open space under her bed. I didn't comment. I told her to gaze openly and take a deep breath. She was mesmerized.

It's good to get used to open space. Layering adds confusion. Space brings peace and ease.

I said to the woman, "This is the rest of your life, open to all possibilities. You and your husband hit a wall, and you kept trying to go forward. The wall's gone." I watched her relax. I continued, "These things are worthless. What matters is what you feel and where you want to go with your life. You've used clutter as a distraction to your feelings, but it's just made things worse."

She understood. She told me she could feel a breeze in the room. But it wasn't coming from outside, since it was a windless day. I told her it 'was the flow returning to the room. She smiled. Clarity brings joy.

We then went through the stuff on the floor. There were things she didn't like that had been given to her by relatives. She didn't want to get rid of them because she felt it would be rude. So she had placed them under the bed to make them invisible. It's like hiding something under your hat. "I don't see it. It must be gone!" But it still weighs heavily on your head.

If you receive a gift that you don't like, either give the gift back to the person who gave it to you, thanking her but saying it's not for you, or give it away to a charity thrift store. My client felt better giving the items to charity.

There were also a lot of financial papers. One of the main causes of divorce is financial stress. The papers were related to dealing with a property that was causing them headaches. I suggested that she talk to her husband about taking the loss and selling it — this would show that the relationship was worth more than the land.

We did not put anything back under the bed. Almost all of it went into the trash, where it belonged.

EXERCISE

- Treat anything under your bed as if someone had taken a full bag of garbage from the kitchen and dumped the contents there. Head to your bedroom with several sturdy trash bags and a flashlight. It's time to do some excavating. A miner's helmet is good too.

- Get down on the floor and scoop out everything from under your bed. Nothing remains. Take all the archaeological findings and bring them to another room with a lot of open floor space. Spill the contents onto the floor, and sit down in the middle of it. It's important to get things out of their resting places. By putting items in unfamiliar settings, you will be able to easily discriminate their worth. Impartiality means everything when you're clutter busting.

- As you venture under your bed, remember that the stuff you find there is stuff you didn't really want to look at, which means looking at it is super valuable.

- Go through all the items with the most discriminating of eyes. Trust that most of them can be tossed. Keep going until you're all the way through the pile.

- From now on, the space underneath the bed stays empty.

Overflowing Bedside Tables

Let's head back to the couple's bedroom. They each had a bedside table, and both were overflowing. Each had about ten books they were currently reading, plus candy, pens, change, junk mail, magazines, audiotapes, and slips of paper with scribbled notes. Some of these things had spilled onto the floor. This mess was representative of the state of their minds.

If you are a couple and there is that much clutter around you, then it is as if you are sleeping in different bedrooms. Clutter is a distraction. You can't see the other person in the room, and you are not in touch with your own thoughts and feelings. If you are single, the stuff next to your bed distracts you from your life in the moment. It means you are not letting yourself relax in the one place designed for peace of mind.

I said, "There are lots of entertaining things on the market, but when you try to take them in all at once, you lose perspective. You can't even tell what you're feeling anymore." I added that they had gathered their big piles by the sides of the bed so that they wouldn't have to pay attention to each other or themselves. She replied that she couldn't even imagine how to begin to deal with the mess.

I quickly pushed all her stuff onto the floor — she couldn't believe I had done that! I said, "You need to have a spacious, smooth surface by your head every night before you go to bed. Otherwise, you take all this crap to sleep with you every night. You're going to have to get used to peaceful stillness again."

We sat on the floor next to this pile. I told her, "This is what's going on inside your head. How could you think clearly with this kind of noise going on all the time? It would be like living right next to the airport." She was excited and primed to toss.

First went the magazines, which she admitted she wasn't reading. Most people I clutter bust have too many magazines and catalogs. They end up in piles. My clients feel that they should read the magazines, but they don't have the time to do so. Mostly, magazines are a way for companies to advertise. You are open to this attack because you are taking in information, and the ads slip in subliminally. It's much like a virus. Soon you end up feeling you need more things. Cancel your magazine subscriptions. You don't need to stuff your head with any more useless clutter. You bought this book because you are sick of collecting.

I told my client that she could have only one book at a time on the nightstand, explaining that it would sharpen her focus and keep her mind from fragmenting. She agreed. The rest of her books ended up in the family's library. The junk mail went. The letters from people went. The magazines were tossed. We needed a *lot* of recycling containers!

My client kept a journal and an angel figurine on her bedside. She did the same thing for her husband's side of the bed. When she was done, there was calm around their bed. When I asked if she noticed, she smiled. It is helpful if you notice the changes that occur while you clutter bust. It strengthens your ability to discriminate functions and puts you back in touch with your feelings.

- Put this book down and venture to your bedside table.

- Clear everything that is next to your bed. Take these goodies to your backyard. If you don't have a yard, go to a local park. I want you to take this stuff as far away from its usual place and your creature comforts as you can.

- Spill it out onto the grass. This is the stuff that for some reason you like to drag into sleep with you. You think the stuff is important to you, and maybe it is, but it has been in the wrong place.

- I want you to be discriminating about what you bring back into your life. Everything in your house is a guest. Guests that disrupt your true happiness have to leave. Handle each item separately. Feel it. Decide if it supports you now. Toss all disruptive clutter into a nearby trash can.

- Bring back only the stuff that is actually valuable to you now. Place it where it is most functional. Your bedside must stay simple.

"Help, I'm Desperate"

A weak and scared voice on the phone said, "I'm desperate. I'm overwhelmed by the junk in my house. Can you come over right now?" She sounded like she was trapped in a well, crying out for help. Many of my clients are at the end of their emotional rope by the time they call me.

I immediately went over to the family's mansion in the Hollywood hills. Though it was nice on the outside, it was becoming strangled by the clutter inside. I could see this as I pulled up in front of her house and found they had to park their three cars in the driveway because the garage was too full of stuff.

My client looked as though she hadn't had a good night's sleep in months. She was frantic and nervous. As soon as I arrived, she handed the clutter-busting reins over to me. It's great working with desperate people because they are starved for change and very open to it. Their lives have just not been working. Perhaps you can see yourself in this light, if you try.

I took a quick tour of the home, which I do with all my clients. I go strictly on feeling. It's the best way to get the big picture, and it allows me to find the root of the clutter. Once I take care of that spot, the rest of the clutter goes pretty quickly. The root of this client's clutter was her office. It was a tiny room, and most of it was taken up with the queen-size guest bed. In the corner was her messy, overflowing desk. The TV blocked the door, making it difficult to get into the room. Her kids' video games were spread all over the floor and bed.

It was obvious to me that her life was out of control. I knew that once she had her own space, her sanctuary, she'd have stability, and then she could save the rest of the home.

I told her we had to get rid of the bed. It was a billboard for going to sleep and was not conducive to work. She was very happy to hear my words, which signaled that she'd already been feeling that but hadn't done anything about it. This is the pattern for many of my clients. They know what is wrong but are afraid to do anything about it until I confirm that it's okay to. Since I may never get to your home, I'll just let you know right now that it's okay to toss those things!

We dismantled the bed and put it outside by the curb. I suggested that we move the TV out of the room and make her office off-limits to her kids. She felt that would be poorly received, since they used it every day for the Internet and video games. I told her it was her room and that if she didn't take charge of it she would remain overwhelmed and unhappy and her family would suffer. She was the heart of the household. It was clear she got a lot of fulfillment from being a great wife and mother. If she was feeling strong and stable, the family would blossom. I was speaking to her strong, compassionate side. She finally agreed. We moved the TV out of her office, and she went to the kitchen and told her kids. They reacted negatively and said they wouldn't allow it. She was discouraged. I took her outside and told her she had to be strong because she and her family would benefit.

She went back and told her kids with strength and certainty that it was her room and that's how it was going to be. They were surprised but went along with her decision.

The woman was glowing. She went to the garage and got three framed paintings that she had bought herself a long time ago and had hidden away. She brought them to her office and we put them on the walls. In an hour's time, this woman experienced a dramatic transformation. She had changed just a few things but was reaping huge rewards. She took back her space and the power that she had given to others. Her dynamism was the evidence of her return to clarity. The nervousness and anxiety were gone. Peace of mind took their place. She now had determination, and over the next week we clutter busted the rest of the house.

Get reacquainted with your space. Give yourself the patience and time to do the work. Identify the areas that feel most personal to you.

As you take a closer look you begin to feel that there's a string tied to everything you own, the other end of which is triple-knotted around your heart. Subconsciously, you are pulled in many directions by the things you own. You become overwhelmed and lose your clarity. This is one of the main reasons so many people are agitated and stressed. While you are in that state of mind, it becomes impossible to separate what's clutter and what is *now*. By going from item to item, you're able to cut one string at a time. That's what makes this process doable.

EXERCISE

- At your home, do what I do when I first come to a client's home: take a tour.

- Carry a little notebook and a pen. Walk through your place as if you were taken there by a real estate agent and you're considering buying or renting the place furnished. Be sensitive to the environment, as if you've never been there before. You now have sensors that will alert you if something doesn't feel right. Be aware of rooms or areas of a room that feel uncomfortable, places where you don't like being. This is an absolute sign of clutter.

- Notice whether some object keeps grabbing your attention, if something feels out of place. If so, it is clutter. The reason may not be apparent, but as with the fridge analogy, you know when something's spoiled.

- Mark the items in your notebook and, when you're done with the tour, go back and clutter bust them. Or remove the items when you see them.

Start feeling the benefits now. I figure that 75 percent of the things in a person's house are clutter. It helps to keep this in mind during the clutter-busting process.

Like Mother, Like Daughter

My client was a single mother raising a teenage daughter. The mother had a tower of clutter. Her bedroom was crammed with clothes and lots of other stuff. I couldn't imagine how she was able to fall asleep amid the noise of all her things. The mother wanted her daughter to be involved in the clutter busting.

The daughter had her own clutter habit. Her room was a jungle of odds and ends that were made to look like art. On one wall were hundreds of photos of her, charting all the "important" moments of her life, from babyhood to the present day. It was like a movie of a character's life showing on five hundred screens at one time.

The daughter's closet was so full that clothes were spilling out onto the floor. However, the daughter wasn't interested in clutter busting and declined the invitation. So I went to work with her mother. We began by clutter busting the mother's clothes closet. While she was letting go of her things, the mother was rabidly complaining about how she'd been asking her daughter to clean up her room for years.

I said, "By the looks of your own bedroom, maybe you were actually saying it to yourself." The mother stopped and took in a deep breath. She started to laugh.

She said, "I taught my daughter all she knows."

I said, "When you're hard on your daughter, you're being hard on yourself. Maybe as you let go of the clutter, you can let in kindness. It's much easier to live with."

Amazingly, as the mother clutter busted, the daughter was off in her room, spontaneously doing her own clutter busting. A few hours into the busting, the daughter surprised us with three bags of clothes she had tossed on her own. The mother had released her clutter of being obsessed with her daughter's life and focused on her own life instead. This had a resonating effect that allowed real change to happen. When you take care of your life instead of trying to care for the rest of the world, life becomes simpler.

EXERCISE

- If you have a child, invite him to help you clutter bust. If you don't, ask a friend if you can "borrow" her child. Tell the child that in the same way we clean and renew ourselves each day, we also need to clean and renew our homes. We need to take an honest look at what we have and decide what no longer fits us — like the shoes we wore when we were two.

- Have the child ask you questions about the value of your stuff. Let his observations reach you. Follow his advice.

- Make sure to pay the child when you are done. In this way he will learn the value of helping people and of service. Plus, this process will help you appreciate your child's voice.

What Matters in Your Life?

On the average, most people own more than a thousand things. Yet you can use only one item at a time. This struck me one day when I was getting ready to go for a drive and went to my CD collection to pick out some music to play in the car. I had more than two hundred CDs. I looked at the throngs of CDs on my two CD towers and was overwhelmed. There were too many choices. The choices blocked any real clarity about what I liked. I was looking at the result of impulse buying. That day I thinned out the music collection to twenty-five essential CDs. The criterion for keeping a CD: I would be happy to listen to it at any time.

Clutter busting is about doing the opposite of acquiring everything you think you want and need. It is about putting a stop to the unhealthy process of acquiring things with the idea that they will make you happy. But I'll say it again: *No thing is going to make you happy.* You may think it will. But the mind is not reliable as a source of good solutions. It bases its decisions on fantasies, repressed desires, and fears of the future based on past events. It is basically impossible for the mind to see the current moment for what it is.

To stop acquiring and start assessing is key. Look at what you have and ask, "Does it help make my life better, or can I let it go?" It's not about standing in an empty room and finally being happy. It's about deciding what matters in your life. What's important to you? Not to anyone else. There's no room in your life for other people's opinions. Self-reliance is crucial. That's why it's important that you question what you want. That's why I ask my clients, "Do you need this, or can we let it go?"

There's so much more flow in this reverse process. It is physically and emotionally easier to adapt to change than to resist it. Most people don't realize this. There is great joy in living a life that is always fresh and new. But we are told, through advertising and brainwashing, that it is not enough. We are hypnotized to believe we need things, that we must have "joy enhancers." I am telling you to go the other way. To live with, rather than to resist, change will give you continuous contentment and joy.

Are You Buried Alive Under Paper?

A writer hired me to clutter bust his apartment. I was amazed at the amount of paper that greeted me when I arrived. There was paper everywhere, creating hills and valleys over the floor and furniture. It looked like a piece of environmental modern art. The disorder was so intense, it was hard to think. My thoughts became jumbled and chaotic, and it wasn't even my stuff. I imagined what my client must have been feeling. He told me that he'd had "major writer's block" for six months. He could write nothing creative or coherent. This is a symptom of clutter. He knew I could help him clean up but didn't see how I could help with the writer's block.

We started with the sofa, which was covered with layers of junk mail, receipts, fast-food wrappers, and pizza boxes. We went through each thing, piece by piece, tossing every item. He was surprised it was so easy to let these things go. Sometimes it takes another person's eyes to help you see. By reading what I've written to you, you now have a second pair of eyes to help you see what is in your way.

When we got to the bottom, we saw that the seat of the

sofa had caved in. The spring was broken, and he had piled paper on it to cover it up. "Hey, if you don't see it, it's not there!" Imagine what your hidden clutter is doing to you right now.

We agreed to toss the sofa and carried it out to the sidewalk. The amazing thing is someone came by and took it after we went back to his apartment. Next we ventured to the floor, which was a mess of fast-food wrappers and boxes. Confident now that he had tossed the sofa, he easily let the floor clutter go.

His "desk" was the next remarkable item. He had his computer monitor set on a cabinet of drawers. The monitor was precariously hanging over the edge. There were papers stuffed under the monitor and spilling onto the floor. It looked like the computer had been giving birth to paper.

He had an old dented and rusted filing cabinet next to a cabinet, and this supported his printer. He informed me that this haphazard computer formation was where he spent most of his time. No wonder he had trouble writing! He was writing in a garbage can. He had allowed the clutter to paralyze his creativity.

I told him, "You'll never create anything worthwhile until you appreciate your skill. Writing in filth diminishes your capabilities. It's time you admit you are worthwhile and have gratitude for your life." I suggested that he get a proper desk and clean up the papers.

He agreed, and we went through the papers. He didn't care for any of the writing, and he threw it out. We then went to an office supply store, and he bought a three-tier computer desk. We brought it back to his place, cleared a space, and assembled it. He put the computer and its accessories on the desk. He was transformed — like someone who threw out the same dirty clothes he'd been wearing for ten years and was wearing a brand-new colorful outfit. His place was cleared and clean, a blank slate, and he had a new direction. I left him to explore the new terrain.

When I called my client a week later, he told me he was able to complete a writing project he had been working on for months. He also had some great new creative ideas and was excited to see where this new momentum would take him.

EXERCISE

- Find the place in your home where you have layered clutter. Clutter attracts other clutter, and where there is some, there is often quite a lot more hidden underneath. There are things in this pile you have been putting off. Over the long run, putting something off causes much more pain. It's as if you bought something on sale with a very-high-interest credit card and spend five years paying it off, and it ends up costing three times the sale price. Now is the time to use your new discriminating eye to find and toss the clutter.

Since you have gotten this far in the book, I know you have the momentum to do this. Go through each item in the pile with a discerning eye. You have been living in a trash can. You have hired yourself to find and toss the trash.

Clutter Busting Your Mate

As we saw with the story of the client and his writing space, you'll stay stuck until you create the space in your mind and home for clarity. More stuff doesn't help. You need the space for the knowing awareness to become a part of your life so you'll make beneficial decisions. This was the case with another client of mine. She was in desperate need of clarity. She asked me to take a look at her place and give my expert clutter opinion. My client greeted me at the door and led me into the apartment. Her home was overflowing with artwork. It was like an art museum, but with five times as much stuff. I felt as though each piece was competing for my attention. "Look at me! No, me, me, me!"

She told me that her husband was always working and that she had a lot of free time to create art. She was very lonely. I recognized that she unconsciously created art and put it on the walls as a way of getting his attention. But since the art was giving off such a needy feeling, I felt it had the opposite effect and made him not want to come home.

I told her the art was clutter and was having a detrimental effect on her relationship. There was just too much on display, and it was overwhelming her husband. Space is just as important as the objects in the space. If things get crammed and pushed up against one another, it's unsettling. He needed to experience her in the clarity of quiet and simple space. That's the best way for open emotions to flow.

She told me that her husband had expressed that there was too much artwork on the walls, but that she wanted to make even more and put it up. I said, "You're craving communication with your husband, but you need to be simple and more direct." Looking forlorn, she told me that she tried but it only made him angry. I had a feeling she wasn't telling me everything.

Next she showed me their bedroom. They had a king-size bed, which was butting up against the husband's equally massive antique desk. This was further proof that the husband's attention was focused more on work than on their relationship. I told her that there should be only a bed in the bedroom. The focus of the bedroom needs to be on the couple. She agreed but didn't feel her husband would make the change. I suggested we move on.

We went to the balcony, which was filled with dead plants. It was a mirror image of her emotional state. I told her that if one of the partners in a couple won't listen, then the other has to change tactics. Getting rid of the clutter, the deadwood, allows one's life to regenerate in new and better ways.

I said, "The one thing you can do now is get rid of the dead plants and get new ones to replace them. Deep, rich, green ones." I also advised her to pick out *her* favorite art pieces and take the other ones down. This way she would be doing something to please herself rather than someone else. She would be taking her attention off him and putting it on herself. This would enhance her self-image and make her husband take notice.

I called her a week later to see what changes she had made, and she told me she had done as I asked. Her husband did notice there was more space. She didn't reveal much else.

My client called me seven months later. Her voice was emotional and a little shaky. She told me that she was leaving her husband and asked if I could come over right away and help her move her stuff out of the apartment.

The place was in disarray. All her clothes had been pulled out of the closet and drawers and were in a heap on the floor. Her suitcases were out. She seemed manic but had a strong sense of purpose. She confessed that her husband was a drug addict and alcoholic and had tried to kill her the night before. She used to think that she could help him change. Since the time she had clutter busted her place, she'd regained her clarity and realized he would stay the same. She needed to leave. She was clutter busting her husband.

A lot of anger was being released with her decision. The clutter had pushed it down, but now that the clutter was gone, it was free flowing. She had tremendous energy and seemed very bold, a complete contrast from the last time I saw her. I said, "Pack only the things that represent your new life of strength and freedom. The other stuff we'll give to charity." She was in the perfect state of mind to hear this.

She let go of the things that reminded her of her husband and kept the things that made her feel independent. She tossed about 80 percent of her clothes and shoes. She decided to leave all but two pieces of artwork. Since she no longer needed his approval, she didn't need to keep the needy attention-getters.

Two hours later we had packed up both our cars, and we drove away from there. We moved all her things into her new safe house. As we unpacked, she tossed even more things that did not represent her new life. Her life had been a lie, but now she had broken through the death grip of her clutter. This took tremendous courage and resolve. She didn't know she had this kind of strength. It all began with the simple realization that she had been living under a shroud of clutter.

I trust you are beginning to instill this same sort of honesty in your life by reading these stories of people who were able to make such tremendous changes.

EXERCISE

Clutter extends past paper and other inanimate objects. People can also be clutter. You may have relationships that no longer fit you. At one time they were an important part of your life. But now they can go. You're also freeing the other people up to move on.

- Get out a pad of paper and some color markers. Draw a figure of each of the people in your life, and write their names underneath. Lay these pages out on the floor.

- Consider each page and ask whether these people invigorate and contribute positively to your life or deplete and add unnecessary weight to it. You'll know right away. You have that innate discriminating mechanism.

- Send the people you will keep in your life their drawing with a nice note attached, telling them that you are grateful for them. People love to have drawings of themselves!

- Toss the drawings of people who you have decided are "clutter." And then either tell these people it's time to let go of the relationship, or let the relationship drift away naturally.

EXERCISE

- Let's take another walk through your home. This time keep an eye out for things that are calling for your attention, things that want you to notice them.

- When you find them, ask, "What do you want

me to know?" The answer may take any form: a feeling, a thought, a physical sensation, an insight. Or you can just toss the thing.

There is no one answer in clutter busting. It's a very personal process. You only have to listen.

Celebrity Clutter

I got my first celebrity client, and I was pretty excited. I wanted to see if she had the same kind of clutter as everyone else. I went to her home high up in the Hollywood hills. The house, at first, seemed immaculate. It was a beautiful space with very nice furniture. She led me into her office and showed me her files. There was a tremendous amount of paper clutter. It turns out that celebrities are not immune! We took out all the files and started sifting through them. We tossed a lot of junk.

During a lunch break she told me she was pregnant and feeling tired and overwhelmed. Sadness was brimming in her eyes. She said she was feeling guilty about not being very productive. She wasn't able to achieve nearly as much as she was used to achieving.

I said to her, "You're not doing anything? Hmm, let's see. Today you created three billion strands of DNA, something science still barely understands. A spinal column. An immune system. Plus, you maintained your baby's heartbeat. So I guess you could be a little tired." Her mouth hung open. She shed a few happy tears, then laughed. Her inner clutter of evaluating her worth based on her ability to achieve the high standards she set for herself had diminished her clarity. When she took an honest look at what was happening in the moment she got her clarity back and she instantly felt joy again. Months later, she called me. She had delivered her baby and was enjoying being a mom. She told me the last months of her pregnancy had been easy because I had helped her view her life from a better perspective. As a result she'd been easier on herself in many new ways.

A Present for Mom

Sometimes a client's feelings are so strong that they overwhelm her and she loses perspective. With the diminishment of clarity the feelings show up as clutter in her living space. This was the case with a client who gave me a tour of her home so that I could see what needed clutter busting. Her home was sparse and orderly, until we got to the guest room. The floor and bed were filled with overflowing boxes. There was no room to stand or sit. She told me her mom was coming to visit the next day. She had cleaned up the entire house and put all the clutter in the guest room, where her mom would be staying.

I said, "What are you are trying to tell your mom?" She didn't get it. She didn't see what she'd done.

I said, "Your mom is coming to visit you, and you decide to clean up and move all the clutter into the room she'll be sleeping in."

She realized and said, "Oh, my God!"

When I asked her how she felt about her mom, she said, "She's always so negative. No matter what I say, she says it's a bad idea or that it won't work out. She never supports me."

I said, "This is your unconscious way of telling your mom, 'No more!' Your communication will be much more effective if you put how you are feeling into words. Then you can be sure she understands. And you'll be giving her the opportunity to change. If nothing else, this is the perfect opportunity to let go of your need for her approval."

We are initially unaware of our clutter. My client had suppressed her feelings about her mom. But they showed up in other ways, and it took an outsider's perspective to make her see it. By reading about others' experiences, you are developing that perspective. You can now use it on yourself.

My client was able to let go of all the clutter in the room. When I called her a week later, she told me she had had some powerful discussions with her mom. Her mother hadn't realized the effect she'd been having on her daughter, and together they started to rebuild their relationship.

EXERCISE

- Imagine that you can have only five items. You have to let go of everything else. What will you keep? Why?
- Now imagine you can get something new if you get rid of one of the five items you kept. What would you like to get? Which of the five items are you willing to get rid of? Can you let that item go *now*?

Jail Cell

Your living space is often the one place in your life you have control over. Thus it is an accurate barometer of the state of your mind. I find it amazing to see the way people live when no one is watching them. When you are in the privacy of your own home, you create your own laws about how to live. It is your big chance to be king or queen of a country. It doesn't matter that it is small. It's yours. And anything you say goes.

Then I show up and challenge the kingdom and the way it runs its affairs. This causes some confusion, and the king or queen dispatches the armies who show up to defend the territory. This is when I get to hear excuses about why the place is like it is and why it should stay that way. These armies bluster a lot, but they are standing on flimsy ground. After a small round of questioning, they fall apart. The monarch is deposed, and freedom returns to the land. This brings a spontaneous way of living that allows and encourages new ideas and flexibility.

I had a client who was the queen of her apartment for twenty-two years. She complained bitterly about her home. Then she complained that she would never move out. It felt like a prison from which she could not escape. When I asked her why, she went into a diatribe about her vast array of health problems and how they had kept her from doing pretty much anything for more than twenty years. So in a way her body was an even smaller jail cell. The thing is, there were no jailers around. No one told her she had to stay.

Her apartment reflected the inner mess. It looked like she was growing a crop of boxes. There were many stacks, piled five boxes high. There were the additional crops of tall, uneven piles of paper, jagged outgrowths of miscellaneous books, and five vacuum cleaners.

I knew that by going through these weeds and yanking them out, she would release the clutter in her mind. I said, "You are living in a field of weeds. There's no room to breathe. This trash that you have everywhere is keeping you rooted in this place. We've got to clear it out if you want to get out of here."

She told me she needed the stuff. I replied, "That's what my clients say about something that is holding them back." I asked her when she had last looked in her boxes. She couldn't remember. I told her I could help her move, but we'd have to toss the stuff that was no longer useful to her. She didn't see how it was possible. I assured her, "Of course it is; otherwise, you wouldn't still be here. Let's go through the boxes."

I did a quick sort through her stacks of chaos. The items were mainly health related. The majority seemed to be endless records of every doctor's appointment she'd been to in the past twenty years. They were filled with her chaotic scrawls.

I said, "We can let these medical papers go."

She said, "No, I need them. I need to know the reasons that I'm sick."

I asked, "Are they going to make you well?"

She did not want to talk about this.

I said, "You're sick because you don't want to get well. Otherwise, you would have answered yes. These papers are your reminders that your physiology is broken. You have a lot invested in these; that's why you are defending them so strongly. You've brainwashed yourself that you are a sickly little girl; that's why it seems impossible to go the other way, toward being healthy and happy. Letting these go is the first great step toward the freedom you tell me you want."

I don't think anyone had ever been this blunt with her, because she couldn't respond. The physicians certainly hadn't told her this. She was their gold mine.

Her armies regained their footing. She whined, "I'm sick, okay? I don't feel good. I'm in pain all the time. I need these things."

I asked, "Do they make you feel better?" She was confused. She never thought she could feel better.

She said, "I'm sick. I don't feel good. There's nothing I can do about it. I don't want to do this anymore."

I asked, "If there was something you could do about it, what would you do to feel better?"

Again, she couldn't say anything. There was profound silence. We were tearing down the walls of the inner clutter fortress that was keeping change from occurring.

She returned, but with less passion, saying, "I really, I don't know, I just, I don't think . . . I'm sick, okay?"

I said, "What if there were no doctors? What if there were only you? What if you got to make all the decisions about how things should be? What would you have happen?"

She became calm. The mental fires were gone. She quietly said, "I would be well."

I said, "Great decision. How does that feel?"

She had the beginnings of a faint smile.

I asked, "Can we let go of the opinions of other people, so that you can start to heal and feel better?"

Together we let go of multiacred fields of weeds. I could feel her internal conflicts ceasing. Gentleness was taking over, like the calm after a ferocious storm. This is freedom. The clearing took three days.

I called her a month later, and she informed me that her health problems had rapidly diminished and her outlook on life had brightened. I reminded her that she had done this for herself. She had realized there was a problem and moved in the direction of change. For the rest of her life, she would do very well by continuing to ride this wave of change. She also informed me that the apartment building she was living in had been sold. It was going to be turned into a condo. As an incentive to leave before the lease was up, the owner offered her $10,000. She took it and was now happily looking for a new place to live.

EXERCISE

- Go to the worst pile of clutter in your home. Declare yourself the Official Name Giver to clutter structures in your home and name the mountain. The Amazing Pile of Crap! The ·

Tower of Shit! Barb's Shrine of Confusion! Harry's Hellish Heap of Hodgepodge! Lovely Litterpool!

- Next, pretend you are a tour guide for this famous spot. "For eight years, nonsensical items have made the decision to nest here. Feel free to root through the endlessness and find your own very special piece of treasure!" Go through the items with this lighthearted attitude and toss the things that don't have a place in your life anymore.

Have fun with this. Humor is a great way to gain new insight. It releases the old way of doing things.

An Overflowing Garage

Sometimes we hide clutter because we feel that if we don't see it, it's not a problem. But it diminishes our clarity as much as clutter in plain view does. That's why you see garages so often featured in these pages! A woman called me to come help her clutter bust her garage. It had been packed with the greatest of efficiency. It's amazing how well people arrange their clutter, so it looks good. "Hey, if it looks good, how can it be clutter?" Yet she and her husband couldn't walk through the garage, let alone park their cars in it. The clutter was almost to the ceiling. They kept the garage door down as a way of not having to take care of the situation.

Other stuff often needs to be stored in the garage besides cars, like tools and paint, but for the most part people's garages end up becoming huge waste bins. They are the elephant burial ground for clutter. Things get pushed there, out of view. This usually means that whatever ends up in the garage no longer fills a need in the person's life. But since the items are still in the home, the people remain attached to them and don't want to face tossing them.

People's garages are like museums of artifacts from their past. Many people have these museums. Take a walk down the street and look into people's open garages. You'll see piles that take up a whole wall or corner or the entire garage.

If you have stuff piled in your garage and you don't believe that it is worthless to you, answer this question: Would you ever leave your wallet or purse in the garage overnight? I figure people subconsciously wish someone would break into their garage one night and steal the crap. They'd be surprised and relieved.

My client and I began the archaeological dig of her garage. We investigated some boxes that were filled with mildewed clothes. These were beyond repair and were tossed. Behind the boxes we discovered three rows of pristine *National Geographic* magazines. They were a huge wall of bright yellow. She told me it was her husband's collection, which he never looked at, and she hated that they were there, but she never told him how she felt. Her jaw was clenched. This is the kind of clutter that destroys clear communication between a couple. I told her to call her husband

and tell him how she felt. She called and told him that she wanted to toss the magazines. I heard him on the other end of the line yelling back at her that they would stay. She yelled back that she was tossing them, and then she hung up on him. She told me to get rid of all the magazines, and I put them in boxes and began carrying them to the curb for recycling pickup.

Her husband worked a mile away from the house. He must have left right after she hung up because he came racing down the street, honking his horn.

He was yelling out the window of his car, "What the hell are you doing? Put those back in the garage!"

She yelled back, "I'm throwing them out!"

They had a full-blown argument in their driveway.

I let it happen because I knew a lot of clutter was being released from their relationship. I was standing at the curb with a very heavy box of *National Geographic*s.

A neighbor drove by, stopped, leaned out his window, and asked, "What's going on?" The husband explained. The neighbor offered to take the magazines to give to his daughter's school, and I carried the box to his car hoping to make that happen. However, the box of magazines burst in the middle of the road. The asphalt turned yellow.

The husband started to laugh, one of those deep, gut-busting laughs with tears. It was his final release. He saw how ridiculous the situation had become. He agreed to let the neighbor take the magazines.

Intuitively, I knew the husband had initially resisted letting go because these magazines were his sanctuary. He was the president of a very big company. He was a workaholic. He never took time off, and the magazines were a fantasy. They represented adventure for him. It was the *idea* of adventure he was preserving. He didn't know this. It was unconscious. Since he never looked at them, they didn't help him. But when they were threatened, his deep desire to get away was threatened. That's why he got angry.

When you deal with your clutter, realize that your reasons for having the clutter are often unconscious. You may get to the bottom of them, or you may not. The main thing is to let things go that are not useful to you now so that clarity can be restored to your life.

The husband decided to take the rest of the day off and joined in the clutter-busting session with his wife. His wife remarked privately to me that she had never seen him so happy and smiling. He probably prevented a future heart attack. By the end of the day they had evicted most of the useless items from the garage. Things that were broken were thrown away. Things that still had some use were put in a large pile for charity pickup. They were able to put both cars in the garage. They couldn't believe their accomplishment.

EXERCISE

- Can you park in your garage? If you can, is it a tight fit? I've learned to assume that most stuff in the garage is crap. A car is okay to have in the garage. Tools for the car are okay too, provided they are for the car in the garage and not for a previous car.

- I want you to drag the clutter out of the garage. Bring it out into the light of the driveway. Imagine you are cleaning out a morgue. You want to get rid of the feeling of morbidity. You want to feel happy in the garage. Go with the feeling that the clutter traffic is a one-way flow, out of the house permanently.

- Go through the things with your now very powerfully discriminating eye and mercilessly toss the clutter into your garbage cans or dumpsters or bring them to a charity right afterward.

- When you're done, pull the car into the garage. It's the car's room. You wouldn't want other people's clutter in your room, would you?

Buried in Email

Computers are just like garages. Many things get stored and organized in these (virtual) contained spaces, and like garages they are often trash cans that rarely get emptied. They are stuffed with emails, folders, programs, and photos that are no longer useful. You don't clearly see their distracting effect as you would a hallway so packed with clutter that it's difficult to walk through. But the clutter in your computer trips you up in ways that greatly reduce your clarity by disturbing your peace of mind and thus your effectiveness.

It's valuable to see your computer as having space. In the same way your home has rooms, so does your computer. When you are checking your email, you are in the email room. When you are surfing the Internet you are in another space. When you create a folder on your computer's desktop, you have created a new room. All these areas have functions that can assist you. However, when your email room is cluttered with unanswered or old emails, or when your computer's desktop space is flooded with outdated and extraneous folders, you are influenced by the clutter in these spaces and are operating from a chaotic and overwhelmed state of mind. You end up creating problems for yourself. Life doesn't function smoothly. You can't think clearly.

The computer is supposed to make our lives easier. Yet many of my clients have computers that are in disarray, and so are their lives. They are embarrassed because they think something is wrong with them. Or they push themselves harder in an attempt to make things work. There is nothing wrong with them. They have simply adapted habits that disrupt the flow of life. It is possible for them to interact with their computers in a way that serves them and makes their lives better.

Your computer needs weeding, just like the rest of your living space. Weeds are anything in your computer or the way you interact with your computer that is making your life difficult and frustrating.

I was working with a client in her home office, and she was complaining about being overwhelmed by her email. She got over a hundred a day. She told me she spent two hours a day trying to keep up with them and she wasn't able to. We opened up her laptop and looked at her email account. There were hundreds of emails on the screen, and as we were looking at them more were coming in. As she witnessed the emails increasing in front of her she gasped, "Oh, my God." She looked frail and ill.

Emails are an odd thing. If you had one task in front of you to take care of, you could complete it. But when you have a continuously growing number of things to take care of and you can't keep up, it's like an assembly line that's moving faster than your ability to complete the tasks. It reminds me of that *I Love Lucy* episode in which Lucy and Ethel are trying to package the chocolates on the conveyor belt and they can't keep up — they have to cram the chocolates in their mouths and stuff them down their shirts!

I closed her laptop. I asked her to take a breath. I had her look out the window at the bright blue sky. I said, "It's easier to think like this. When everything is simple we think clearly. We're going to go back into your email account with this new point of view. It's good to know that emails are letters people sent you. They are important to those people, but they don't have to be to you. They are asking for your attention. It's your attention and you can choose where to put it. You have only so much to give, so we are going to make choices. You will decide what's important and what isn't."

I opened up her laptop. The first email we looked at was from a friend who regularly sent her political emails. She said she felt compelled to read them and respond. She also said they agitated her. I said, "If you didn't respond to your friend's emails would you be okay?" She relaxed and said yes. She wrote her friend and asked her not to send her the emails.

We moved from one email to the next. Because we approached it from the perspective of "is this important to me or not?" she was able to think clearly and make decisions. She responded to the ones that were important and deleted the ones that weren't.

If there is clutter on your computer, that's an indicator that it would be helpful to bring awareness and clarity into interacting with your computer. It's a simple thing. It's slowing down and stopping to take a look. You're looking at how you feel when you are using your computer. If something agitates you, if something worries you, if you feel yourself resisting something on your computer, it's time to look and make a decision. "Is this important to me and making a difference in my life? Is it something that I need to take care of and then delete? Or is it not serving me and I can delete it?"

At one point my client didn't want to respond to or delete a particular email and instead wanted to put it into a folder. I asked to see her email folders. She had a multitude of them and was embarrassed. She put things in folders because she didn't have it within her to face them. The thing is, even though they were hiding in a folder, a part of her knew they were there, and this bothered her.

I said, "We're noticing that the idea of the folders doesn't work for you. The folders don't assist you. Let's go through these and see if any of this information that you set aside and stored is valuable to you or not. And if not, we're going to delete it."

We took a look at her files. She had stored a large number of articles that people had sent her. The senders thought they were interesting. She respected these people more than herself and stored them. The evidence that she hadn't read the articles meant they weren't part of her life. They were clutter. She said, "I'd feel guilty deleting these."

I said, "It's good that you recognize this. Guilt is clutter. It doesn't propel you into action. It doesn't help you finish things. It punishes you. It won't make you change your behavior." She looked awake and strong. She deleted the folders.

Your computer is part of your personal environment. It's as much a piece of your living space as your bedroom, kitchen, living room, and bathroom. As with these other spaces, it's important to see how you feel when you are in your computer's space. How do you feel when you are working on your computer? Do you feel good after spending time on it? Do you find yourself getting lost, spaced out, while you are on it? Do you feel anger or resentment or despair when you are looking at your email? Do you feel like you can never catch up with what you need to do? When you are done working at your computer, do you feel drained? Do you feel like you wasted your time? What part of interacting with your computer space do you enjoy?

The world can be a needy place. It will always have something to ask or demand from us. The computer is a communicating device. It's an extremely sophisticated phone. The world continually asks for our attention by calling us through the computer. We need to attend to it in a way that supports us. It's important to take care of our responsibilities, and one of these is taking care of ourselves.

A wonderful way to take care of ourselves is by listening to the still, small voice within us. It tells us what we need. It lets us know when we are overwhelmed and need a break. It informs us when we need to take action. It gives us intuitive ways of taking care of business. This voice is as much a part of us as our hearts and brains. It's the voice of clarity. When we are unhappy or frustrated or overwhelmed, this is the voice letting us know that the way we are doing things isn't working. We don't have to stay on the assembly line. We can step back. This greater awareness creates more space. This space provides clarity. And clarity presents solutions.

EXERCISE

- Sit in front of your computer with the computer turned off. Feel the chair below you. Be aware of how relaxed your legs are. Look at the blank screen. Notice your reflection on the screen. Take a breath.

- Turn on the computer and watch it warm up. Imagine that you woke up your computer. It's stretching. It's happy to see you. It asks how it can help you. Tell the computer how you would like it to assist you. Let it know that you want to clean it and remove things you're not using anymore. Ask for its assistance to see what's no longer serving you.

- Go to your email account and check out the inbox. Go through each email and decide if you need either to respond to the email or to delete it. No maybes. Maybe means something is bothering you and it seems like it would bother you less to ignore it. However, it affects you more when you leave it undecided.

- When you have cleaned out your email inbox, take a break. Get up and walk around the room. Take a look at the floor and the walls. Notice what's going on outside your window. Drink a glass of water.

- Go back and sit down at your computer. Now go through your email folders. Go into each one and delete any messages that you no longer need. If the folder is empty, delete it. The amazing thing is you'll notice that you feel better when you get rid of any folders that aren't part of your life anymore.

- Go through your email contacts. Find the names of people whom you no longer are in touch with. Delete their addresses.

- Take a look at your favorites or bookmarks list. This is the list that links you to websites you felt were important to visit again. See which ones you are no longer visiting and delete them.

- Stop and walk away from your computer. Stretch. Get another drink of water. You're doing great. It feels amazing to let go of things that don't matter to you.

- Come back to your computer and take a look at the folders on your desktop. This includes photo folders. Open each folder and honestly ask yourself if you need the information in the folder or if you can let it go. This is similar to going through your fridge and seeing what food is old and tossing it in the trash. Remember that when you let something go that's not part of your life you allow the space for something new and better to come.

- When you are done, thank your computer. Then say good-bye and shut it down. Sit with the computer and watch it shutting down until the process is complete.

Chapter Seven

INNER CLUTTER CREATES OUTER CLUTTER

As should be abundantly clear by now, outer clutter is caused by inner clutter. Let's look at this phenomenon more closely. Inner clutter consists of unconscious emotions, the ones you purposely ignored and then forgot — something that was overwhelming to you in some way. But when you ignore something, it becomes bigger because it feeds off your attention. Purposely not thinking about something holds your attention. When you ignore something, you're actually still thinking about it. You just happen to be thinking that you should not be thinking of the issue! Doing this requires an amazing amount of attention and energy.

Imagine a buoy floating on the surface of the sea. To purposely keep it below the surface you have to apply force, pushing it down. And you have to continue applying force to keep it submerged. In the same way, if you're repressing something emotionally, you have to keep it submerged, just below your conscious awareness. This requires the constant pressure of distraction. Distraction often takes the shape of items you bring into your life that you would normally never acquire but that you got because they temporarily distracted you from your feelings.

The problem with distraction is that it works only for so long. You get used to the thing. It no longer shines. So you have to get another thing. Then you have to get another thing. These can be things you bought in a store, or got from a friend, or found. They can be people who in their own way are distracting. It can be a project you unconsciously started doing because of its distracting abilities.

This is the definition of clutter: things that exist in your outer life to distract you from the inner things that you're avoiding. If you avoid something, it grows. Something small can end up becoming the size of Montana. The great thing is, the reverse also holds true: when you honestly look at something, it shrinks. When you see the situation for what it is, bypassing the emotional layers that colored it and made it into a clutter monster, it becomes simple. That's how peaceful clutter busting is. You're honestly looking at each layer of distraction, questioning the thing, letting it go, and realizing what's underneath. Looking directly at something has the power of a magnifying glass in the sun. The sun is you; the glass, your attention.

Taking an Honest Look

Your honest nonjudgmental awareness will allow you to see the fruitlessness of your inner clutter, which in turn will allow it to be spontaneously released.

When you are filled with inner clutter, the chaos reflects in your personality as obsessiveness, confusion, disorganization, broken speech patterns, insomnia, indecisiveness, and lack of direction. When your home and world are in disarray, you can't relax. It takes more energy to be in chaos because you have to keep track of all the junk. Eventually exhaustion sets in. When you honestly look at clutter and ask if it's necessary in your life, buried emotions come to the surface. You may start thinking about things you haven't faced for years. Toss what's unnecessary so that you can finally relax, and your remaining possessions will have a clear place to land.

Let's go back to the fridge-cleaning metaphor. Imagine you are sorting through the items and find a dozen eggs forgotten for two years in the back of the fridge. They would, of course, smell. When you look at your emotions honestly, they are released and the clutter gets tossed. Sometimes it's replaced by a big smile, and sometimes tears of letting go. If you start to feel a rush of emotions, remember that *inner clutter causes outer clutter*. You are tossing out the trash.

Release Your Creativity

Inner clutter has a way of cramping people. It cuts them off from what's inside them and directly inhibits the flow in their environments. This was true in the following case. I got a call from a gentleman whose wife and baby son had been away for a month and were returning in a few days. He had to clean up the place before they returned. He sounded panicked, so I went right over.

The basement fascinated me. I noticed a big crib with three huge, vintage electric guitars precariously hanging over the top. The guitars felt like dragons hovering over the crib, threatening its occupant. There was a feeling of competition for available space. Right away I knew that he was feeling that the baby was imposing on his creativity.

I asked him how often he played the guitars. He looked sad. He said that he used to play every day and that he used to be in a band. But since his son had been born, he had not been able to play the guitars for months.

I took one of the guitars off the hook and handed it to him and asked him to play me a song. He plugged it into an amp and started wailing some great blues rock. He came alive! He went from pale and sullen to vital and passionate.

I said, "You're a very creative person. You need to include creativity and art into your day, along with taking care of your child and being with your wife; otherwise, your time with your baby and wife will suffer. You'll see them as impediments to what you really love doing. Instead, you can love your family and music as a great daily mixture. Since you want to be a good dad, you need to feed yourself too. Then your kid will grow up learning that part of being successful is being kind to yourself."

He was touched to realize he could be responsible *and* happy. He said he would play every day for a half hour or so. And he would have his son listen to him.

His son would be his inspiration.

He then revealed to me that he and his wife didn't like the crib. It was a gift from his sister, and they didn't want to tell her that they didn't want it. I suggested, "Tell your sister you don't like the crib and give it back to her." He told me she got angry easily and he was afraid of how she would react.

I asked him, "If your sister knew you felt this way about the crib, do you think she'd want you to keep it?"

He said, "She'll say, 'I got it for the baby. Why can't you use it?'" He shrank as he said this and looked pale again.

I told him, "You're living in fear of your sister. Having the crib keeps that fear alive. Do you want to go on living this way, every day for the rest of your life?"

He was still apprehensive.

I said, "Imagine your son is your age and he is too timid to speak up for himself. Do you want your son to learn to be afraid to speak up, like you are now?"

He said no. I said, "This thing you are doing with your emotions right now is clutter. It is getting in the way of you enjoying your life. It blocks your creativity and your heart. It doesn't serve you, and you can let it go. Think of it as pivoting, making a simple change of direction toward something that will benefit you. It will make you stronger." He took in this information with a deep breath. I could see the resolution in his eyes.

My client then called his sister. He told her that he and his wife didn't need the crib and asked her if she could come by and get it. I could hear her complaining through the phone. She was loud and angry.

He stood tall throughout. He persuaded her to come and get the crib that night.

When he got off the phone he seemed naturally stronger with a sense of certainty and resolution. He had clutter busted his fear and moved forward in his life.

We took apart the crib and put it out in the driveway for his sister to pick up.

We rearranged his basement with some simple changes that made it creativity friendly. We took the guitars off the walls and put them on floor stands so they were easily accessible. We took two paintings he had done but hidden away and hung them on the wall. He said he felt like he was breathing for the first time in years. He also said that he was happy to soon be with his family because an essential part of him that had been missing would be included. It's a wonderful experience to see a person's essence shine through when their clutter is removed. What part of yourself would you like to infuse into your life and living space?

No Broken Stuff Allowed

When his wife and son returned, my client invited me back to clutter bust their house. I was able to watch him and his wife interact. She was Japanese, and he was not. She spoke only a little English. He did not speak Japanese, so they had a hard time communicating. What they wanted to say was not communicated properly. It was a source of frustration for them both.

He and I went upstairs to clutter bust his office. There we found a photo of an old lover. He told me that it had been a demoralizing relationship, and he was emotionally pulled back in time. My client started to look smaller, paler, older.

He told me he'd had many bad relationships with women, each one causing him to have some kind of a breakdown.

I told him the photo and the attached memories were clutter. He became defensive and did not want to throw the photo out. When a person is trapped in his past, he acts out of emotion. It's hard to reach him, as if your messages have to travel back in time. I'm patient. I know that sometimes you have to go around an iceberg to get past it.

I was immediately drawn to a waterfall machine on his desk. When I asked him if it worked, he said it didn't. He turned it on, and the waterfall made horrible grinding noises. No water flowed. I asked if it could be fixed. He said no. I said, "It has to go." He refused.

I said, "You've got to toss broken things. Otherwise, they spread, like a crack in the windshield of a car that eventually spreads across the entire windshield. Broken things cause disorder in your home. You don't need that. You need the harmony." He angrily said, "No, Brooks, it stays!"

I asked him where he had gotten it. He revealed that the waterfall was given to him by a woman he used to see, someone who helped cause a complete mental and physical breakdown that had lasted three months.

I suggested that eventually he would lose his current relationship too, which shocked him.

I said, "If you keep this living symbol of a bad relationship in your home, you keep it in your heart and it grows and destroys what is good in your life. You'll have no room for love for yourself or for anyone else. It's up to you."

My directness sank in. He was deeply reflective. Then

he picked up the waterfall machine and tossed it in the clutter busting trash bag. He looked triumphant. He did this for himself.

My client then went to a secret compartment in his filing cabinet. He brought out a thick stack of photos of all his old girlfriends. On his own he tore the photos up, one at a time. His eyes were filled with tears. He looked like a sick man becoming well before my eyes. A lot of clutter grief was released. This was amazing and exciting to watch, because I knew he would never be the same.

We continued on with papers in his files. A half hour later his wife came up to the office to see how the clutter busting was going. Suddenly they were communicating very easily. They spoke intuitively to each other to make up for the language differences. They were very loving toward each other. She left to let him get back to the busting. He told me how amazed he was that they were able to speak to each other so easily. I told him it was the result of his letting go of his old relationship clutter. He had cleaned out his inner clutter, and his life was vastly improved.

EXERCISE

- Sit quietly. Think about something that you've held on to a long time that you haven't used. It was important to you at one time and doesn't fit your life anymore. But you still have it.

- Think about how much better things will be when you let it go.
- Toss it and sit quietly again.

How does it feel now that it's gone? What difference will this make in your life?

The Hope Chest

Another client of mine had suffered from bad relationships in the past. She told me that her greatest hope was to find a good partner and have a family. But her life was littered with failed relationships. As a result, she spoke of her desire with fear and doubt.

I noticed a special chair in her living room, which turned out to be an old birthing chair. There was a big old *Vogue* magazine sitting on it. It looked like a cranky old vulture that kept anything good from sitting there. I told her to get rid of the magazine if she wanted to have a family. I was allowing her to leave open the opportunity. *Vogue* and similar women's magazines sometimes make women question their worth. Trying to look like a model (a physical impossibility for most women) drives many women to eating disorders and deep levels of unfulfillment. It's a common source of clutter for American women.

I then zeroed in on the bedroom, a great barometer of someone's intimate life. I went under the bed to look for goodies. There was an old, beat-up leather suitcase lying in wait. When I pulled it out, my client's eyes went wide with dread. I knew I'd pulled out a really large corpse. She told me it was her hope chest.

The suitcase was stuffed with artifacts. I asked her about all the contents. There were many old boyfriend relics. They were from relationships that ended badly. She was not on speaking terms with any of the men. She looked nauseated and uncomfortable.

There was a painting done by an ex. The painting was wrapped in swaddling clothes. She looked ill as she related the horrible, gut-wrenching details of the relationship's demise. She pretended that she needed to keep the painting because one day the artist would die and it would be worth a lot of money. I felt as though she wanted him to die because of the pain he had left her in. I suggested that she was poisoning her life by having this under her bed. She went to sleep every night and then stewed in her past pains for a good eight hours, as if she were in an emotional Crockpot. That's why she was eating the dreadful soup of her lonely and sad life. She further defended the painting, saying that it's important to hang on to art.

I asked her, "What's of greater value to you, owning a plain and dull painting by someone you don't care for, or having someone new in your life who adds freshness and love and vitality every day? Fresh and vital love is worth more than money. But it's up to you." She let the painting go. She lost about twenty pounds of emotional weight.

Next I pulled a broken pipe out of the suitcase. It was a

peace pipe given to her by an ex who had died from a drug overdose. There were tears in her eyes. She was still in mourning. I told her, "The way you are feeling now is what you feel every night that you sleep over this memory of sadness. Is your life worth more than this? Do you think we can move this out? Keeping the pipe won't keep him; it will only keep the sadness resonating in you. You want an open, free heart. Otherwise you won't have the room for any kind of living love." She didn't say anything. I could feel her grip loosening.

I said, "If nothing else, do you want the symbol of a broken peace pipe to represent your life? That's what it's doing now. It's up to you. You can let go of these things so your life can spring forth." A look of awareness crossed her face. She gently took the peace pipe and put it in the trash.

I spoke with her a week later. A new man had entered her life. He was gentle and kind. She even related the story of her clutter busting, and he was glad she told him. She was in the midst of an opportunity for real love in her life.

Think about my client's story. Are you living in a graveyard? Is it what you want? Memories of the past can capture your attention, but how much fun is that? If you're living in the cemetery of your past, that means a great big part of you is dead. But some part of you is still alive: your essence, the pure feeling of existence.

When you move the corpses out, you shine forth. That's what you've been going for all this time. It's the reason you shopped and acquired and held on to things —

because you wanted to feel alive. Loosen your grip. Let things fall away. You'll look and feel a million times better.

Career Clutter

The inner clutter people feel can also create chaos at their jobs. Late one evening I got a call from a client who needed me to come over right away. I'll go to work whenever people realize their life situation is an emergency, any time of day. I'm the clutter fire department.

My client lived in an amazingly small studio apartment. Her floor was littered with dirty laundry. Most of the pile was lingerie and rubber bondage items and leather fetish boots. She was a famous fetish model. This is someone who poses in this stuff, tied up and mostly naked.

Her career was laid out on the floor in disarray. I knew that she was experiencing great emotional inner clutter about her job. She didn't know how to resolve her situation.

In her tiny kitchen was a huge heap of more leather and rubber boots. I asked her if she wore any of the boots, and she told me she had never worn any of the foot items because they are fetish "collector's items." She wanted to create a fetish boot museum in her little place. She had the planks of wood and the supports to do it. The hardware was sitting in a pile next to the boots.

She told me these things had been there for a year and a half. Then she let me know she had an insatiable foot fetish.

She was erratic in her moods. She threw a dazzling and

scary fit when I accidentally stepped on one of her boots. She told me that her erotica collection was more important to her than people were. She seemed trapped in her space. She was unfocused. Her mind was racing. She was easily distracted. She was twenty-one, and she looked thirty-five. These were symptoms, not the real her. I always separate the person from their crap. They are not their crap, although they may think otherwise.

I told her, "This is going to be so easy." She didn't believe me.

I asked her, "Do you like living like this?" She quieted down and became introspective. She looked like she was going to cry. She quietly said, "No. I don't know where to start."

We began by going through the clothing covering the floor. Most of it was lingerie. I suggested we create a pile for dirty clothes and another for clean clothes. She regained her focus. She was on a roll.

She told me she was not comfortable creating order in her life. She sat very close to me and told me she likes older men. She looked deeply into my eyes. She told me she's a sex addict. She reached out and grabbed a magazine and showed me naked photos of herself. My client was not at all sexy during any of this. She seemed lost, as if she were drunk. Her eyes were distant. Rather than face the clutter, she was trying to distract me. It was all right because she was also revealing her inner clutter. I said, "Let's just pay attention to the clutter." She stopped the sexy act.

With her defense mechanism disabled, the inner clutter started to release. She began to cry big sobs into a towel. It was quickly soaked. She told me she couldn't do it anymore — the traveling, the bondage, the whippings, the impersonal sex. She said she felt as though she was raping herself. She felt worthless.

My client told me that she had never said this before. It felt like she had shed her skin. She looked reborn. I told her she could be gentler with herself. She started to go back to her cluttered mind by telling me about the obligations she had to her clients. I asked her if she was bound by contracts. She said no, that her work was freelance. I told her it's good to say no when you want to.

She very quietly said, "I want to say no to everyone."

I congratulated her. I asked her what she wanted to do. She very solidly said she wanted to quit being in the photos and instead produce fetish photo shoots. It sounded like a good idea because it would create a distance between her and her work.

The room felt peaceful for the first time since I had walked in. It was easy to go through the rest of the clothing. She put two big loads of clothes in the washing machine down the hall. We did build the boot museum. The boots looked great on the walls. The footwear was so diverse that it gave the feeling of being in a fun and fancy art museum.

When we were done, she had regained her strength, and she smiled a lot. By getting to the heart of her physical clutter, she was able to release some powerful emotional clutter.

- Relax and let your mind wander. Imagine there's a film coating your life and keeping you from shining. It is acting as an insulator to keep you from certain feelings. What particular things in your life have the dulling effect of this film? The correct answer is always the first thing that comes to your awareness. It can be abstract or tangible: an activity, a belief, a hobby, or anything else that comes to your mind. It can be something you would think of as sacred, that you would normally protect. But clutter is a virus in your home. It has found a way to adapt to your environment and feeds off your energy. It eats at your peace of mind. It deserves to be recognized and rooted out.

Book Trap

We saw how when inner clutter about work is released a person's life shifts powerfully and positively in the moment. The following is a story about how a client's investigation of her inner work clutter transformed her work and mental space. She worked in publishing, and her house was cluttered with books. They felt like vines that had overtaken her home. She said she was okay with the books, but it felt like a defensive statement. Underneath, there was a feeling of being trapped. To admit that would have meant that there was something wrong with her job and, deeper still, something wrong with her life. It was easier to pretend that everything was fine.

I told her it is good to go through everything individually to see the details of what matters and what doesn't. She moaned about it being too hard. The mind resists change. It plays a movie about how terrible it's going to be, even though it might be pretty easy and make the person's life better.

I enthusiastically said, "Oh, my God, this is going to be so much fun! This is so exciting! You are the luckiest lady in the world!" Her mouth hung open. My playful reaction threw her. The attention was focused on a better place — I had given her an invitation to have a good time. This is in itself a clutter busting. She had a cluttered way of dealing with the world, a way of being that she picked up long ago, probably when she was a kid, and she was still using it. "Life is difficult and hard. Change is not easy. Things are okay as they are." It was keeping passion out of her life.

We worked swiftly through the books. With each one I asked if she had read it. If she had, I asked if she would reread it. If not, I encouraged her to let the book go; otherwise, she would be storing memories and encouraging herself to live in the past rather than living fully right now. When we came across a book she hadn't read, I asked if she wanted to read it. She surprised herself by finding that she didn't want to read many of the books she owned.

She said, "I don't understand why I thought I wanted to read all these books."

I said, "You liked the idea of having the *opportunity* to read a lot of books. It's your desire to have more opportunity in your life. Otherwise, life seems very rigid to you."

This was unsettling to her.

I said, "This is a great opportunity for you. You get to discover what you don't care about anymore. You're opening yourself up to discover what you really do care about." She revealed things about her job that were bothering her. She told me about her hostile boss and his unrealistic expectations. She had been afraid to speak up, going with the status quo. She recounted the changes she wanted to make at work. I said they sounded like good ideas, and she was surprised. She had been thinking her ideas were crazy and would be instantly rejected.

I asked, "What are you going to do?"

She answered with certainty, "I'm going to talk with my boss tomorrow."

I told her, "There are going to be a lot more great changes coming in your life. You trained your eye today to see what is valuable to you and what is not. You got a new skill, and you put it to use. You can keep using this tool."

We brought the books she was letting go to a local charity thrift shop. We went back to her house and arranged the remaining books by category on her bookshelf.

There was a lot of extra space. She had a few pieces of art that she had always wanted to put out, but there had never been any space. We spread them out on the shelves.

The room was transformed. It was a thing of beauty. I checked in with her a week later. She told me that she had called her boss and told him her concerns about situations at work, specifically about her work relationship with him. He listened to her and appreciated her feedback. He told her that she was valuable to the company and he wanted to find ways to make sure she was happy at her job. She was stunned. It's amazing how the damage caused by inner clutter can be swiftly repaired by bringing awareness and the appropriate actions into our lives.

Clutter Brings Out All Emotions

I got a call from a woman who said she wanted to trade her massage services for clutter busting. When I went to her home, I was greeted at the door by a nasal-stripping ammonia stench of cat pee. I was still outside on the porch. I couldn't imagine it was physically possible to go inside.

She didn't apologize about the odor. I figured she was used to the stench. People get used to their clutter and aren't aware of its destructive influence. I mustered up my courage and plunged in. Once I was inside, my sinuses and lungs felt like they were on fire. It was very hard for me to breathe. Hot tears streamed out of my eyes. My nose wouldn't stop running. A three-hour hot oil body massage in the nude given by three bikini beauties would not be worth this. I asked her about the cat problem. She told me one of her cats had a kidney infection and had been peeing on the carpets, walls, and sofa for a couple of months.

Here's what her home looked like: the floor was a waste disposal for books, papers, trash, and empty cardboard boxes; the sofa was piled with junk past the height of its back, spilling onto and merging with the mess on the floor; and clothes in the bedroom were piled onto the floor and any open surface, looking like colorful haystacks.

I asked her about the empty boxes. She told me they were for the two cats to play in. These cats ran across the floor in mad dashes as if they were being chased by phantoms. When they were still, they shook in nervousness. One of them peed on the couch. The woman did nothing about this and sighed. She seemed more concerned about the cat.

I reminded myself to hold on to compassion. Owing to the state of my lungs and sinuses, I had to act quickly.

I asked her if she liked the couch. I already knew the answer. When someone covers up something with clutter, it means they don't like it. She said she hated the couch. She then revealed that she hated most of the furniture. When I asked her why she kept it, she told me that most of the furniture in the house belonged to a previous roommate. He had moved out a year ago and had not come and taken his stuff. She had called him numerous times about when he would come and pick up his things, and he would get angry and yell at her and said that he couldn't at the moment. She felt guilty and was too timid to tell him to come and get it. She was repressing her feelings.

I told her, "The cats are peeing on the furniture because you hate that the guy won't come and get his stuff. You are being taken advantage of. The cats are expressing your feelings and they won't stop until you call him and say that he must come and get his things now."

She was afraid of creating an uncomfortable situation for him.

I said, "This guy is making your life inconvenient every day, every second. This crappy furniture is in your way! Your life won't get better until you get it the hell out of here. Stand up for yourself! No one else is going to!"

She got on the phone and called the guy. She told him that he needed to come and get his stuff. I heard him angrily say, "You're just going to have to wait." I shook my head. I gave her the "you can do it" face

She pulled herself up and told him she was putting all his crap on the curb. When she hung up she was beaming. She had faced her clutter, and it was a triumph for her. Even the cats stopped racing around.

She wanted the furniture out of the house immediately. I got out the trash bag for recycling, and we tossed all the papers on the couch. The couch was ugly. It was a dull gray with plenty of cat piss stains. We carted the couch out to the curb. This was followed by two lounge chairs and another couch. When we got back into the house, she started screaming, "The cat's escaped! Oh, my God! Oh, my God!" She was panicked and couldn't move. I pictured the cat running free, looking back with a grin, "I'm free, I'm free."

Intuitively I went into the backyard and found the cat. It was running away from the house. I scooped up the cat and brought it to her. She grabbed the cat so hard that its eyes bugged out. It looked at me with an expression of desperation and hopelessness. We went back into her home. She made sure the door was closed and locked before she set the cat down. The cat ran into the bedroom and hid under the bed.

Clutter busting brings out all the emotions. Go along with them, not giving them much attention.

I got her a glass of water and made sure she drank it. I recommend you drink a lot of water when you are clutter busting your stuff. I joked with her that screaming was a very thorough form of exercise. She laughed.

I said, "This is what living deep in clutter does to you. You still have a lot of old feelings stored up in you. All this crap on your floor and in your bedroom distracts you from what's going on inside you. Are you ready to let the rest of the crap go?"

She enthusiastically said, "Let's get rid of this shit!"

The old roommate called back. He complained that he couldn't come by and pick up his stuff. She hung up on him again.

We clutter busted the stuff on the floor. She was like a vacuum cleaner. Everything went into either recycling or donation bags. Her strength was back. Mostly I was just holding the trash bag open and getting a new trash bag ready. We moved on into the bedroom. She got rid of at least half her clothes. She didn't like them, so she wasn't going to wear them. There was no going back.

I called her a few weeks later. The old roommate had come and picked up his stuff that day. He was grumbling, and she slammed the door on him. She got a new sofa and chairs and kitchen table. And the cats stopped peeing on the furniture.

- Is there anything in your home that you don't like? I don't care if you spent a lot of money on the item, or if someone gave it to you, or if it belongs to someone else. This thing is clutter. It is junking up your life.

- You must transport the item out of your house now. If the thing is huge, you have twenty-four hours.

From this moment on, you'll never be the same. Acquiring objects for the purpose of experiencing indefinable joy has begun to lose its hold on you. Oh, my, what's going to happen to you? You'll probably start to smile for no reason, and you'll start to feel satisfied without having to do anything in particular. Things will lose their allure. Just the feeling of being alive will be good enough. I guess you'll just have to adjust.

Canine Clutter

We've heard about cats and clutter; now let's give dogs their due! I had a client who had three dogs that were always fighting — a big and slow yellow Lab, a feisty Rhodesian ridgeback puppy, and a tiny mutt of some kind. They were animated chaos clutter. Just like the piles of things around the house, they constantly distracted their owner, who was jittery and apprehensive. When their fighting got particularly aggressive, as it often did, he would yell at them. He loved the dogs, but the situation was breaking his heart.

He admitted the little dog was the cause of the agitation. The little guy would constantly bite at the rear legs of the bigger ones. This made them bark and growl in defense.

I asked if he had tried obedience school. He had. He said he had tried everything, even herbal remedies. He was in emotional agony over this. Since the little one was the agitator, I asked if he could let that dog go. He said he couldn't imagine doing that. He was attached to the dog, even though it was causing him pain. He'd been living like this for three years. The dog was clutter. I told him that as much as he cared for the little dog, he and the dogs were constantly tortured by the situation. That is not love. It's attachment and suffering. If he loved the doggies, he would do what was necessary to make them happy. If the little guy went, they would all be happy. If he did nothing, the fighting would continue and probably get worse.

He had never looked at the situation like this. He saw the truth and knew that he needed to find a home for the little dog. I suggested he call a few friends and let them know the situation. Perhaps one of them would be interested. He had begun calling when one of his friends came over. She was in the neighborhood and had decided to surprise him. As they stood in the hallway chatting, the little dog came into the room and sat on the woman's feet.

He told her that he'd decided to let this dog go. She

immediately said she wanted him. When I called my client a week later, he told me the house was peaceful. His two dogs were calm and happy and playful. I asked him how he was. He told me he felt that way too.

- What do you have that conflicts with the rest of your life? That haunts your house? This item can even be part of your lifestyle. You may have told yourself you love this thing, but if this item causes you distress, it's clutter.
- It's time for this thing to go. Letting it go shows self-love. Sacrifice it for something that brings greater glory into your life.

Home as a Map of the Mind

Sometimes the clutter in a person's heart can be so interwoven into her living space that it can seem normal to her. She can't distinguish what is essential and what isn't. She just knows she is in pain and can't figure out how to feel joy again. One of my first clients was a sixty-three-year-old woman who had somehow managed to squeeze the contents of her previous house into a one-bedroom condo. There were no pathways. There were stacks of things that we had to maneuver around, as if we were in an obstacle course. Magazines were stacked on top of boxes, which were on top of furniture. Clothes were strewn on some of these moun-taintops like snow peaks. Two cats lived in this mini-metropolis of clutter. I couldn't see a whole cat. Just a tail or peeking eyes.

My client never had anyone over. She went to work and came home and stayed there until it was time to leave for work again. While she talked about her life, her eyes had a dull haze. She was living in a world of memories. She looked like a talking mannequin.

People's homes are a map of their mind. The mind is a storehouse of memories and opinions and beliefs. Because it's rare that anything new gets in, the mind becomes stag-nant. Clarity is lost. Problems ensue. Things pile up unused. Her home had become a stagnant pool.

When you toss things and readjust your living space, you readjust your state of mind. I knew she needed a lot of readjustment, so I got out the trash bags and enthusiastically jumped into clutter busting. The first layer of clutter was women's self-improvement magazines, which she wanted to keep. I asked her when she had last looked at them, and she couldn't remember. She wanted to hang on to them because she felt they could help her. I told her she was okay as she was; it was her place that needed renovation. She liked that and said I could recycle the magazines.

Next came the books that were bestsellers in the seven-ties, mixed with stacks of old, musty, yellowing newspapers. There were also plenty of new-age books on how to im-prove your life. These books are common with clutter clients. I told her, "I want you to have a clear living space so you can start to hear and trust your own insights about your life, rather than other people's opinions about what you should do." She let that sink in. She nodded her head and quietly said, "Yes." With this new conviction, she let go of all her self-help books. She wanted to keep the newspapers, though. She felt it was important to document history. I told her there are plenty of people who do that for a living and that if she wanted to change jobs and become a historian, she could hang on to the papers. She let them go.

There were more than eighty books. She'd read only a few. She wanted to keep the ones she hadn't read in case she decided she wanted to read them.

I said, "So you don't want to read them?"

She said, "No, not really." And she let them go.

As we approached the next pile of clutter, she got a phone call. She answered it, and it turned into a chitchat call. This happens with some clients. They use it as an excuse to avoid clutter busting.

I told her, "I need you to get off the phone now." She was embarrassed and hung up.

When you're clutter busting, don't answer the phone. Be cautious of distractions. Your mind will latch on to anything to avoid change. Even though she was off the phone, she seemed somewhere else. People themselves can become clutter. They become a warehouse of unresolved issues. Their minds never shut off. They incessantly go over and over feelings about past events. They are possessed by their memories of the past. What gives me enough compassion to help is knowing that underneath all those cluttered layers, just as in my clients' homes, is a quiet and peaceful place. You can think of that the next time you're around someone sinking under the weight of their painful thoughts. You're not seeing them. You're seeing their clutter looking back at you through their eyes.

I asked her, "Are you having fun?"

This brought her back to the moment. She admitted that she liked tossing things.

She said, "I have something to show you." She brought me into the bedroom.

She got out a bag of tools and started to dismantle her bed. It was a thick, heavy wooden frame. I helped her remove the mattress and box springs. Underneath were six huge overflowing boxes of books on tape: mystery, romance, horror, and self-help. She had listened to them all. I asked her if she wanted to listen to them again. She hadn't considered this. She said, "Um, I don't think so." I said, "Great, let's toss them." She said, "No way!" I said, "You just told me you didn't think so. I'm going along with what you really want." She pouted.

I told her, "If you keep them under your bed, it's like sleeping above a railway station. You're really thirsty for peace of mind in your life. That's why you had all those self-help books. Letting these tapes go will make a significant difference in your clarity."

Some part of her was resisting. She looked very uncomfortable.

I continued, "You've been keeping the tapes because they represent the life you want to live. You want romance and the thrill of adventure and horror, and you want to love yourself. By sleeping above these every night, you get a very slight resonance of your desires. But you're fooling yourself. This ends up making you long for these things and makes you sad. The way to start living the life you want is by tossing out the things that are in the way. These tapes are in the way. They are not the real thing." She couldn't say anything. She was holding back big tears. I said, "We can do whatever you want with these tapes. It's great that you showed them to me. It took a lot of courage."

Her tears began to stream. She held her head to steady herself and cried spasmodically. She looked like a hot air balloon that had dropped its lead weights.

She took my hands, still crying, and said, "They can go."

I even shed some tears, the feeling of relief was so huge. I immediately bagged up the tapes for donation.

Once people let go of something, I move quickly. I don't want to give them the opportunity to change their mind. When you are clutter busting your place, once you know something is clutter, quickly toss it. For this woman, the tapes under her bed were the heart of her clutter. By letting them go, she was transformed. She took over the clutter-busting process after this. She went through her place like a human vacuum cleaner. She was tossing faster than I could keep up.

By the end of the afternoon, forty-five bags later, we were done. We disposed of the recycling in the proper containers and dropped the rest of the stuff at a charity. She seemed mighty. She felt good about her life.

EXERCISE

- Go through your home pretending that you are a detective and you're looking for clues: What are this person's secret ambitions and desires? Take good notes. Remember that things are often symbolic of a desire.

- When you've identified the desire, write it in one sentence and set it in front of you.

- Take a look at your desire. Is it important for you to have in your life? Will it make your life more enjoyable? What can you do about it now? It's your decision. No one knows better than you. Rather than feel your desires from a distance, you can begin to live them. Living what you love gives your life vitality and real joy.

Once you are clear about your new intentions, let go of any representations of your desire that you have never used or haven't used in more than a year. This will impel you to move forward in an exciting new direction. Your home has shown you what you value most.

Chapter Eight

MENTAL CLUTTER

As we saw in the last chapter, the clutter in your mind is the source of all the clutter in your home. The disarray in your mind reproduces itself in your environment. Your home and life are carbon copies of the activity in your mind. If there is chaos in your brain, it will be in your home. If there is peace in your mind, your home will be a joy to live in.

I wrote this chapter to help you start to see the clutter in your mind. Observing the mind's operations will distance you from the erratic and dysfunctional. With this distance, clutter will begin to disappear, and order will be restored. If you just go in and try to fix it, the mess becomes worse; that's trying to cure disorder with disorder. Silent observation, on the other hand, puts things right. Plus, it gives you a chance to laugh at yourself rather than feeling lost and depressed.

Mental clutter comes in various shapes and sizes. Below I'll discuss some of the most common and easiest to recognize.

Being Negative

Our minds have been trained to change or fix things with the use of negative commands. For instance, the number one way of trying to get someone to feel better about a problem is to say, "Don't worry." The problem is that your subconscious mind does not hear negatives; it's deaf to "don't."

If I say to you, "Don't think of a pink elephant," what do you think of? A pink elephant. When you say or hear "Don't worry," your mind remains worried. "Don't get in an accident," "Don't forget this," "Don't forget to call," "Don't do that," "Don't be late," "Don't think that," "Don't hurt me." Take the *don't* out of all these, and what do you get? A life that remains cluttered with difficulty and problems. Positive commands work more simply and powerfully. "Be careful," "Remember," "Have fun," "Be on time," "Enjoy." These types of statements have a lasting effect. It wouldn't help if I said to you, "Don't think negatively." It would be more inspirational and effective if I said, "Now's a great time to let go of the mental clutter and experience living more positively." This kind of clarity is gold.

Complaining

Avoid complaining. When you complain, you carry trash around in your head. You are stuffed with clutter. By complaining, you have let the problem invade your mind and spread like a virus. The more attention you feed it, the more it grows. This habit distracts you from seeing a solution. The best solutions come out of silence. They come from quiet mental space. If you can't do anything about the problem, let it go.

Criticizing

Once when I was working as a bartender, I started to notice a consistent pattern in my patrons. Behind me was a huge mirror. People would order their drinks, and they would look at themselves in the mirror as I prepared their drink. They would squint as they looked at their bodies. This meant they were focusing in on one part. And they never smiled. They seemed unsatisfied. Rather than taking in their whole bodies, they picked out something like their hair or stomach or arms or butt and took the critical eye. The mechanics are this: your mind takes a situation that is neutral, basically okay as it is, and begins to break it down and distort it. It picks out details and magnifies and inflames them. Your mind turns something into a problem. As these problems accumulate, they become clutter and distract you from what is really important.

Anything that you analyze in pieces will inherently seem wrong because you are not taking the rest of the situation into consideration. Your mind creates an illusion, and you suffer. This form of mental clutter is a habit. It can be changed.

When you find your attention narrowing and the criticism beginning, remember to take a deep breath and relax. This will disrupt your critical pattern. The best way to break a habit is to constantly interrupt the process with silent awareness.

Clinging to Ideals

Another kind of clutter worth tossing into your trash can is your *ideals*. Ideals are what we have picked up and adapted from other people about how best to live our lives. They are other people's goals. And often they are impossible to attain. Almost everything we claim to believe we got from others in some way. People in positions of authority sounded good, and we bought into their way of seeing things, in the same way we buy things we don't need from the store.

We rarely look to see if this way of seeing feels good and suits us. We want something because we have been led to believe we're not enough as we are. We don't ask why, so we are left open to needing something that captures our attention and says just the right thing. As a result, we have been constantly striving to achieve some sort of ideal that we're not even conscious of, and therefore we feel frustrated because either it's not right for us or it is unattainable.

To identify the ideals that are running your life, complete these statements:

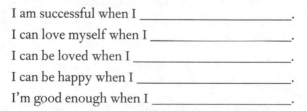

I am successful when I _____.
I can love myself when I _____.
I can be loved when I _____.
I can be happy when I _____.
I'm good enough when I _____.

Your happiness and self-confidence have been dependent on fulfilling these ideals. This means you can't be happy until you've crossed these finish lines. They are clutter because they limit your life. They cause you grief and sadness. They keep you living in the future, which means you can't enjoy this moment. Awareness of these ideals is the first step toward self-acceptance. With it comes relief from the pressure of trying to change your true nature.

When I clutter bust, I ask people a few questions about their lives, and they offer up the things they are frustrated about. Most of them are striving to live a particular way. When I ask them why, they usually don't know. They just feel it's the right thing to do. If you don't know why you're doing something, step back. Refrain from doing it. It's most likely clutter.

When you start tossing out the items in your home that you don't need, you start to recognize the concepts and ways of thinking that don't suit you anymore. Recognizing them, like finding someone in a game of hide and seek, is enough. It will allow change to happen spontaneously.

Collecting Worries

Like many people, you probably collect worries. Your mind is trained to think that if you dwell on all the possible things that can go wrong, you will be able to deal with them if they arrive. This puts you on constant alert, which exhausts your mind and body. You allow these worries to pump a lot of anxiety-producing chemicals into your bloodstream, and over time your mind and body become debilitated. This condition makes you less able to respond to difficult situations. When you've collected a large number of worries they become fretting. Fretting happens when a series of worries repeatedly cascades in your mind. "What should I do?

Should I do this, or should I do that? But what if this happens? What will happen to me? What am I going to do? This couldn't have come at a worse time. What am I going to do?" This kind of thinking exhausts you and gives no positive results. You can change. I did.

I once went to an ATM and got out a hundred dollars. Then I went to the store to buy something. At the register I opened my wallet, and the money was not there. I realized I had left the money at the ATM. I went back thinking it might still be there, but the cash was gone. I tensed up and felt anxious. "Oh, no. I lost money. I'm so stupid. I needed it. Now I've got less money. What's going to happen to me?"

My worries were suddenly interrupted by the thought, "What if the hundred dollars was an admission fee for the rest of the day?" With this came a sense of calm and peace. I thought, "This is pretty nice. I could go back to my worries, but they make me feel pretty lousy. I want to go with the joy of the admission fee." I dropped the pain of the worry and adopted the new perception.

I felt like I had made a good purchase. I had the feeling of being in a theme park.

All the cars were parked along the street for me to look at. All the trees were planted for me to enjoy. My apartment felt like it was set up for me to experience pleasure. Things I normally took for granted became special. The worry habit was clutter busted. What took its place was peace of mind and fun.

I didn't need any *thing* in this state of mind.

What you worry about happening rarely happens. This means worry and fears are clutter. Be aware of when you worry. Feel it. You'll be amazed at the things you've been worrying about. Watching them gives distance, and you can start to think clearly. You get a new perspective.

Procrastinating

Procrastination can come from worry. You avoid taking action when you are worried about the outcome. The funny thing is that the avoidance itself often creates a negative outcome. When you take an honest look at worry, it can be humorous. Your tormenting thoughts about a possible problem can actually be the cause of problems. Now, that's something to worry about!

Thinking of the Future

Your mind becomes cluttered with thoughts of the future. Sometimes it's as if your life *right now* is insignificant compared to what might be coming up. The future is not guaranteed — *anything* can happen. But your thoughts dance around things that may or may not happen with the anxiety and anticipation that they will. These thoughts are clutter. They do not enhance your life. If you look at what your mind predicts as the future and what actually happens, you will see that the mind is most often wrong. So getting caught up in thoughts of the future is like hiring a financial analyst who is constantly wrong and continuing to listen to and pay him.

Worrying about the future takes you away from the

beauty of *now*. The things you have now are things you had to work hard to get. They were once the things you eagerly anticipated. But once acquired, they lost their shine, and your attention shifted to what to get or do next.

Worrying about the future allows tension to filter in, lessening sense perception.

Remaining open to now creates clarity and calm and a readiness for anything. If nothing else, know that *anything can happen* in the future. There are innumerable possibilities, ones that you can't even think of.

Why do we clutter our minds with thoughts of the future? The underlying reason for the odd activity of obsessing about the future, as we touched on earlier in the book, is the deep-seated fear of death. If you see yourself in the future, you are reassuring yourself that you will remain alive. It's a rickety, false fantasy of immortality, since the future rarely turns out as you expected. It is a trick you use to give yourself a sense of stability. We already know the truth about stability.

You must clutter bust that backward way of thinking. You don't need it. You take care of yourself handsomely when you are alert to your life right now. If you go back to the future, ask yourself: How good a future is it going to be when it finally rolls around and I am still focused on the future?!

The ever-changing world is forever a surprise. If everything happened as you feared it would, life would become maddeningly dull and depressing. *Then* you would have a problem.

Butting In to Others' Lives

We are obsessed with other people's lives, especially their problems. This is a way to avoid being responsible for our own lives. It keeps us from enjoying our lives and is therefore mental clutter.

Often clients will veer off from their clutter busting and passionately and angrily talk about the details of another person's life. They sound erratic, their eyes become glazed, and they tend to ramble. Their train is off the tracks. They are showing me one of the sources of their state of disorder.

I had one client who, in the middle of tossing her junk, went off on a rant about a particular couple's relationship with their child. She felt they were improperly raising their son. Her voice got louder. There was a lot of pain underlying her words. At the emotional height of her spouting, I interrupted her and asked, "Why does this mean so much to *you*?" Her attention was shifted from the couple, the outer clutter, to her feelings, the inner clutter. I could see the realization come to her. She quietly, vulnerably, and powerfully said, "Because *I* want to have a baby."

She relaxed. She was surprised by what she had said. She had tossed something that wasn't serving her, and this was intuitively replaced with something that meant a great deal to her. She was back on track. She never mentioned the couple again. She went back to clutter busting with renewed vigor and insight.

When you put your attention on others' affairs that don't directly involve you, you become depleted of the enjoyment and caring you can extend to your own life. It's misplaced attention. It doesn't help you drive forward. Grab the steering wheel and turn in the direction of your home and your heart.

The mind is a subtle tool. Veer it back in the direction of your world and remember: MMOB — Mind My Own Business.

The Importance of Compassion

The great thing about being silently aware of the unpredictable functioning of your mind is that it brings in compassion. You watch the up-and-down mad antics of your mind and you realize that it wasn't built to be an independent and successful problem solver. It changes its point of focus erratically and debates itself with contradictory thoughts; it's tied into, swayed by, and frightened by the volatile combination of fears, memory fragments, and fantasies; it rationalizes any kind of behavior; when tired it tends to become confused and autocratic and seeks instant gratification; and it's motivated by unconscious emotions that are difficult to assuage.

You feel compassion for yourself when you silently watch the inner workings of your mind. It's quite a show! And you can have a sense of peace knowing that it's not your fault — you were taught by the world that these are normal ways of thinking and being. Most people operate this same way. When you are aware of these attributes in yourself you can understand how it is that you have the outer clutter in your life. This kind of thinking process makes your life difficult. It's noisy and distracting and distorts what is. When you see the culprit, the confused and overwhelmed part of yourself suddenly understands. With understanding comes sympathy.

This compassion brings the space of kindness into your heart and begins to clear the inner clutter. As the mental clutter starts to naturally drop off, it's replaced with an intuitive knowingness that allows you to solve your problems with effective ideas that you've never thought of before. Plus, you experience a greater richness in just being alive. This feeling of fulfillment is what you were seeking when you were trying to feel better by acquiring things. You are noticing it right now in yourself as you read the pointers in this book and test them in your life.

Chapter Nine

CLUTTER AS PUNISHMENT

Living in clutter can be a way of inflicting pain on yourself. Maybe you punish yourself because you think you are not good enough in some way. Maybe you do it as a way of creating an incentive to do better, the idea being that if you create enough pain in your life, you will change. But you don't change as a result. You only get used to the pain, becoming dulled to what you are really feeling.

Creating a Prison

Some people also use clutter to punish others, along with themselves. One of my clients used her kitchen this way. It was a horrible mess. All the countertops and drawers and cupboards were jammed with intertwined chaotic crap. The refrigerator was a traffic jam of old and new foods piled on top of one another. The kitchen table was dirty and piled with books, mail, newspapers, and old food. The sink was piled high with dirty, caked dishes. The room smelled rancid and musty.

I tried going through the individual items with her, but she was unfocused and spent her time complaining about her family. She was lost at sea in her stormy emotions. She complained that her family never helped her and that she was tired of taking care of them. I knew that she felt neglected. She wanted their attention. She had created this environment to punish her family, in the hopes that it would make them see their evil ways, then show they loved her. She only wanted to feel loved.

This was an unconscious act on her part. It's good for you to read this, because many of your actions are most likely unconscious ways of getting a message to someone. Since most people are not aware of your subconscious intentions, they don't get the message and you may get so angry or sad that you are unable to properly communicate your feelings.

To break the grip of her anger and resentment, I took out an especially heavy and stuffed drawer and dumped it out on the floor. Her mouth hung open. I got down on the floor with the stuff and said, "Come on, let's go through this crap." She laughed.

She got down on the floor with me. I quickly asked her about each item. Because she was still a little stunned, she was knocked out of her woeful feeling and able to see what was worth keeping and what wasn't. She ended up tossing most of it. There were only a few pieces of silverware left when we were done.

I got out another heavy drawer and dumped it out on

the floor. She laughed again. This time she seemed lighter, as if her self-distracting burden was gone. She began to take over the process and to toss many things before I could even ask about them. Again, the drawer was nearly empty when we were done. She commented that much of the stuff was worthless.

She dumped out the next drawer. She was on a mission. I said, "You are good at tossing things out. I should hire you. You know it's good to feel important in your own life. You can't always expect everyone else to notice you. You have to be proud of the good things you do with your life, because essentially it is your life. Everyone else is caught up in their lives. It's not that they ignore you; it's just that they are obsessed with their own lives. The funny thing is, people begin to respect and notice you when you feel good about yourself." She stopped for a second and cried a little.

Then she began tossing again.

We threw out the clutter on the countertops and the old food in the cupboards. And then we cleaned out the fridge. She was amazed that most of the food had gone bad. We cleaned the kitchen table and washed the dishes. I noticed that as we proceeded she got stronger and faster. I am always amazed by the dulling nature of clutter and the mightiness of clarity. My client then cleaned off all the remaining surfaces.

Many of you might be tempted to buy organizing devices to store the huge arrays of clutter in your home and in your kitchen. But these are just attractive trash cans. Show no mercy! The trash doesn't deserve your respect. You do!

The days of punishing yourself, and others, are over. Punishment does not deter future negative behavior. It acts as fertilizer for the unwanted weeds. So instead of punishing yourself, praise yourself. Amazing things will result.

Lifting the Clutter Curse

One of my clients was a mom who lived in a big home with her husband and two toddlers. Her husband was gone most of the day producing TV shows. She was at home all day taking care of her babies. The house was a mess. She just couldn't keep up with it. She was exhausted. I told her that in caring for her two kids and husband full-time, she had ignored herself. This had worn her out, and she had very little to give. My client didn't want to hear this. She didn't feel there was time to take care of herself. She was punishing herself.

You end up resenting people if you always take care of them and not yourself. You do it to get their love and admiration, but you end up resenting them, because deep down you only want to be loved as you love them. You feel you are prostituting yourself for the love of others.

I told my client that unless she took care of herself, starting right now, she wouldn't be able to take care of her loved ones, and that they would ultimately suffer; in fact, they already were suffering. The house was a mess, and she was terribly behind in taking care of basic household needs. She had to start with herself, and then everyone else would benefit.

My client cried. Even though she didn't want to hear it,

she realized what she needed. There was a release of frustration in her tears. She had tried to be Super Mom and Wife. This ideal image she had tried to live up to was her clutter. She was punishing herself with the image because she told herself she couldn't take care of herself, she couldn't rest, until she proved she could be this ideal. So the ideal was actually standing in the way of her being a great wife and mother. It stood between her and her happiness.

She agreed to try to take better care of herself, though she was uncertain how.

The first place we clutter busted was the bedroom. It felt off balance. It was too active and chaotic. There was no sense that anyone could rest in there. To keep up with her busy life, she needed to focus on getting deep rest.

Next to the couple's bed was a massive, round table. It took up all the free open space. On the table were a fax machine and an old computer that were not being used. I asked her why they were there. She didn't know (a perfect clue that something is clutter). I asked if she could let them go. She said, "I guess so." All you have to do is ask sometimes! We dismantled the table and took it and the other two items to the pile outside that was going to charity.

I asked her if she noticed the room starting to open up and breathe. She did.

Off in the corner of the bedroom was a small, messy desk. It looked like it was squished into the space. There were shelves above the desk, and things were piled on the shelves all the way to the ceiling. They were threatening to spill over the desk and onto the floor. I asked her what that mess was all about. She looked down and quietly told me it was her office. Her husband had his own big office upstairs. The kids had their own huge playroom. All she had was this miserable-looking desk. Her cluttered and punishing way of putting herself last was diminishing her capabilities. I asked her if there were any empty rooms in the house. She showed me a nice-size empty room upstairs.

I said, "This is your new office space. Let's move your desk up here. You can spread out and breathe again." She didn't think it was possible. I asked if the room was being used for anything else. She said no.

I said, "You're burned out. You have nothing left to give to your family. You need to regenerate to be of any use to anyone. Having your own space will allow you time to recharge. You are the nurturer of this family. If you have nothing to give, everyone suffers. As it is right now, you're not able to keep up with the demands of running a household. You're running the ship here, and you need a captain's quarters."

She liked the sound of that. I took all the clutter off her desk and brought it to the living room. If you try to let go of things in their usual environment, it can feel odd to change anything. You are used to a particular visual pattern. When you take clutter out of its regular home and put it in a new environment, it loses its visual hold. It is easier to see what no longer fits in your life.

Most of the papers were insignificant. Previously she hadn't been clear-headed enough to see that the papers were worthless to her and that she was hanging on to everything.

She had a new clarity, and we were able to toss most of the papers. Then we took the desk and the important papers up to her new room. She seemed uncertain that she was doing the right thing.

I had her bring a portable CD player into her office and told her to pick out a CD of her favorite music. She told me she hadn't listened to music that she likes in a long time. Then she picked out *Billy Joel's Greatest Hits*, mentioning that her husband doesn't like it. I said, "He's not here. Play it." She put it on and turned the volume low. I turned it up loud. I said, "This officially inaugurates your brand-new office. Congratulations!" She danced and sang along loudly to "You May Be Right."

When I suggested that we organize her new office, she said, "Organize," and shuddered. That is a great clutter clue. When you listen to a person talk, the words they say reveal their beliefs. It is the key to how they see the world. Her feelings about organization were keeping her from organizing her life — they were a kind of clutter in and of themselves. When I asked her how she felt about organizing, she said she hated it. She admitted that her mom was a big organizer and was constantly involved in planning activities. Her mom was a workaholic and never had time for her daughters.

I said, "You're nothing like your mom, are you?"

She said "No, not at all." She smiled. She understood. The mental clutter curse was lifted, and we set to work organizing her office.

I felt her strength returning as she constructed her new

office. When we were done, she felt like a general, fully in command.

I said, "It feels great, doesn't it?"

She gleamed. "Yes."

- Take a walk around your house and look for areas that feel diminished, weak, and constricted. Sense areas that seem a little blurry, places where you've slighted yourself.
- Stand there. Ask yourself what you want that you're not allowing yourself.
- The first thing that comes to you is your answer. Just by recognizing this desire, you are planting a seed in very fertile ground. When self-honesty takes the place of self-deceit, the potential for change is released. Listen for ways to begin. Sometimes simple recognition is the necessary springboard to making changes.

Chapter Ten

USING YOUR DISCRIMINATING TOOLS

By now you are more than ready to start clutter busting. But maybe you have lingering doubts about your capacity to do so. The truth is, you are equipped with amazing discriminatory abilities, ready at a moment's notice to distinguish between what is a waste of your time and what is valuable.

All you have to do is ask.

We're used to being told that we don't know what's best for us and that other people are the experts. I'm acting not as an expert but as an inspiration to help you get motivated to use your innate clutter-busting apparatus. It doesn't matter if you don't feel ready; the truth is, your discriminatory machinery is always ready to get you out of the chaos and back into the clarity. Here are some tips to help you fine-tune your discriminating machinery.

Recognize Defense Mechanisms

As we know by now, any time you meet with resistance, you know you are standing on a gold mine of clutter. You have some emotional attachment to an object whose only function is to distract you from what you are really feeling. You don't have to know why it's there, but you can know that the thing is worthless and is interfering with your ability to enjoy your life.

When I ask clients about a certain object and their eyes get glazy, as if they're in a trance, I know the object is clutter. It is as if their eyes are out of focus, as if they have instantly become drunk. They often unconsciously rub their head, arm, or stomach. They sit or stand a little off balance. They tend to speak in disjointed sentences that sometimes trail off midsentence. The flow is gone.

Recognize this manifestation of emotional resistance while you are clutter busting your stuff. This is your defense mechanism in operation. It keeps you from living in the moment and from seeing that something is clutter. Its function is to prevent change. Your clarity is gone. How can you notice if something is unnecessary if you can't see it?

At this point I ask my clients questions to jump-start their minds, their discriminating facilities. You can do this for yourself at the moment of confusion or tiredness or impatience. It's about retraining your mind to get back its edge of discrimination. When you're working by yourself and this happens, when you feel your thoughts have gone off on tangents that have nothing to do with what you're looking at, when you start to reminisce about old feelings, you have hit a clutter oil well. I like to think of it in terms of abundance because clearing out the weeds allows the space for the right crops to flourish. Ask yourself questions about the item's value; watch your mind trying to defend the item. Being aware of the mind's defense mechanisms is great clutter busting. If you help a friend clutter bust and he manifests these symptoms, you'll know you've hit the clutter bull's-eye. Ask questions to help him use his powers of insight again. Don't answer for him. Compassion is a big part of clutter busting. Whether you're doing it for yourself or another, have respect for the clutterer. It helps eliminate the judgment he already has for himself.

You can also trust that when confusion comes up, the item is clutter and you can just let it go. Trust that the signals are correct. It's okay to leave out the intellect, the reasons why you kept the thing. It's good to learn to go with the signals from the heart, a habit that will be supremely beneficial the rest of your life.

Your Home Is Not a Warehouse

Your home needs open space for you to feel peace of mind. But when a large quantity of stuff accumulates or is set aside for possible future use you diminish your ability to think clearly. Top businesses understand the benefit of operating with less. They have been cutting back on their inventories. It's cost-effective and makes business stronger. They don't need to warehouse things because today anything can be obtained by an email or a phone call. Often you can receive items within twenty-four hours.

This applies perfectly to you in your home. You don't

need those extra items that you were saving in case you might one day need them. The mind often worries about things that never happen.

If you end up needing something you don't have, make the call, send the email, or take a quick drive. Allow the businesses to store the thing you need and use their services if you do happen to need it.

In its essence, discriminating is about simplification. Life is simple and requires very little. The mind is complex and has greater needs. Allow yourself to become aware of just how simple life itself actually is. Contrast it to the mind's insatiable demands and desires.

Toss, Then Organize

Discriminating is about making a decision: Is this thing serving my life or not? When you directly ask yourself this question you get an answer: "Yes, it is," or, "No, it isn't." It's simple and effective.

However, many office supply and organizing stores take advantage of people feeling overwhelmed and not able to think clearly enough to discriminate. These stores are in the business of selling you supplies to help you store your clutter, the idea being that if it looks orderly, it's not clutter. But the truth is, if you stack all your crap in pretty boxes and transparent containers you will still feel confused and disordered, and you will probably go and buy more things so you will feel better. I've gone into people's homes that appeared to be very orderly but were still very cluttered. They spent a lot of money on organizing devices that get stuffed with their clutter and become expensive trash cans.

When you get rid of the clutter, you will have a lot more space and you won't need organizing devices.

Create a Filing System

A simple filing system can be much more effective than all the contraptions designed to help you organize. It can help you make easy decisions about where your papers go. Right now your filing system, if you have one, may be a bit chaotic. Perhaps your papers are living free-range around the office and through the house. A clean, simplistic system brings peace of mind. You can follow the same process I use in helping my clients discriminate what papers to toss and what and how to file.

First, I ruthlessly go through the papers on the floor, on countertops and tables, and in the files themselves with the feeling that most of them can be tossed. I help my clients question each piece of paper's validity. I doubt the person's professed reason for keeping the paper. I have to. People think papers are valuable when honestly, most are not. We've been brought up to think that papers are important.

Look at all the attention placed on the report card or test scores when you are in school. The teacher hands you the test *paper*, and there is a mark on it that affects which college will accept you and what kinds of jobs you will be able to get. When bills come in the mail, they often make you fret. And then there's the stigma and fear you place on your tax forms. Heaviness is associated with something as simple and silly as paper. Paper is just wood pulp mixed with water and chemicals. Ink has been applied to the paper in recognizable symbols. Most of the paper you encounter does not deserve being housed and does not deserve a moment of your sympathy. Think of it as an enemy that must be rousted unless, like certain financial documents, it is of absolute necessity.

When I'm working with clients, I keep things very basic and ask, "Do you need this _____ paper, or can we let it go?" What doesn't get tossed in the recycling bin I put in general categories. The general categories are very basic. The clients keep those headings unless the grouping is too big (e.g., "Finances") and needs to be separated into smaller categories ("Taxes," "Bank Statements," "Credit Cards").

If you don't have a filing system and think that they are a waste of your time, know that living without a filing system is like having planes fly around your head without a place to land. They continue to fly around in their circles burning precious fuel: your attention. If these papers don't have a good home, they keep flying around in your unconscious mind using up valuable energy. Build the airport. It's very simple. You'll notice how much better you feel when the planes land and are neatly parked in hangars. Your mind will be freed.

Does It Fit My Life?

When you're nine years old, you might wear a size-three shoe. But when you're ten, your foot is bigger. You can look at the size-three shoe and say, "This shoe is good for me;

look how it's kept my feet safe for the past year." But you're not seeing that it no longer fits you and now hurts your foot. You're using memory, rather than how you are feeling now, as a gauge.

You are probably walking around with size-three shoes and complaining that your feet hurt but without recognizing your shoes as the source of your discomfort. In the short and long run, they're hurting you. The best way to make sense of your life is to ask honest questions about your things. Is this object important to you now? Does it bring you benefit? Is it in the way? Are you saving it because of the memories? Can you let it go? Would you like to have something new and better?

You have outgrown many, many of the items you currently surround yourself with. I know and, more important, now you know that 75 percent of the things in your home are worthless to you.

A Collection of Clarity Exercises

The following are a group of clarity-enhancing exercises that you can do to help you root out and let go of more clutter. As you let go of the clutter you will feel your sense of awareness get sharper and you will enjoy feeling more present.

We get used to things being a certain way and don't notice when they become stagnant. It helps the clutter-busting process to look at your things in a different way. You can discriminate when you have a better viewpoint. Here's an exercise to help you do that.

- Select a category of things, for example, books, clothes, dishes, furniture, CDs. Go through your home as if you're walking through a store and looking at each item in the category.
- Assess each of the items and ask yourself if you'd buy it now. If you answer, "Yes," it stays. If you answer, "No," then toss it. This question is especially powerful with clothing.
- Ask the same question about your car and your home. Maybe it's time for a move?

When you are standing in line to purchase something, you don't think, "One day I'm going to toss this in the trash." But one day you will. It will break, wear out, or outlive its usefulness to you. When you're shopping, it helps to look at even nonperishable things as if they have an expiration date. It could be a day, a week, a month, a year. The following exercise allows you to assess the expiration date of your stuff.

- Access that part of you that can tell when something has spoiled — you know, that part of you that when you open the lid to something in your fridge and smell, knows right away. Go through your things with that spoil radar turned on. Sense what has expired. You'll know instantly. You'll feel an odd sensation in your body, or something will catch your eye as being out of place, or you'll pick up something and immediately feel tired and irritable.

- Once you know that an item's value for you has expired, immediately let it go.

It's hard to think clearly when you are distracted. The following exercise simplifies your discriminating process and makes it easy to root out the distractions.

EXERCISE

- Clear out a room. Leave nothing in it. Then sit quietly in the middle of the room.
- You are the most important object in the room. You experience all the great things in life. You are what stays.
- Now leave the room. Go get an item and bring it into the room with you. Sit across from it. Ask if this item fits your life. If you feel a strong affinity, keep it in the room. If you don't, take

it out of the room and put it in a pile of things to be donated or recycled.

- Repeat this process with the things you own, one piece at a time.

- When you are done, toss out everything that doesn't fit your life. Take the things that do fit and place them in your home in a way that delights you.

You can jump-start your discriminating faculties with creativity. This next exercise allows you to use your innate creativity to discern what really matters to you. When you know what matters, it becomes clear what doesn't.

EXERCISE

- Identify the area in your house that is most chaotic. Go in there with a pad of paper and a pen.

- Pretend that you are a journalist and that you have come to interview the room. Sit down on the floor and ask your room some questions:

"How are you today?"
"How did you get started?"
"What are your secret dreams?"

"What are your favorite things?"
"Where do you see yourself in five years?"
"What's bothering you?"
"Off the record, what do you secretly hate?"
"What country would you like to go visit?"
"What do you wish you could wear?"

- More questions will come to you. Ask them.
- Write down what you imagine the room would tell you if it could respond. Write it all down. Some of the answers may be in drawings.
- Intuitively, you will know what things can go. Toss 'em.

WHAT REALLY MATTERS

Now that you're at the end, welcome to the beginning! This is the start of a new life — one in which you start to really value yourself. Ultimately it is your life to enjoy. It is up to you. What do you have otherwise? A house or apartment that you dread coming home to? A life not worth waking up to in the morning? There is no value in things. The value is in *you*. You don't need anything — you alone are enough. You know now that you were mistakenly taught otherwise. You now know what really matters.

There is a true story about a woman who was working at the World Trade Center when it was struck by terrorists. She ran out of the office with a friend. When they got to the stairwell she said she had to go back to her desk and get her little girl's picture. She never returned.

She went back for a thing, a representation of something that mattered to her.

How could she have done otherwise? We are all trained to act this way. We have been living this way most of our lives.

To live peacefully and happily, honestly look at what you have and ask, "What matters? What do I really need? What is worthless to me now?" Keep what matters. Toss what doesn't. It's easy once you start.

I tell people if I can do it, so can you. My life used to be a mess, but then I cleaned it up. I found I enjoy my life in simplicity. I have more fun than I used to when I had so many things but felt confused and unsatisfied.

Everyone's clutter-busting story is different. Yours will be too. You will find yourself laughing at some of the things you have held on to. You might cry. You will feel joy in tossing things that do not matter to you anymore. You are making room for yourself. In the end you will feel freedom, the kind you have been wanting all along.

Happy clutter busting!

SUMMARY OF CLUTTER-BUSTING PRINCIPLES

- Remember that nothing is sacred except you.
- If it doesn't fit anymore, physically or psychologically, let it go.
- Take the items that you are going to review out of their space and move them to another room, or outside, so you can get a fresh perspective.
- If you hesitate, trying to decide whether something is worthwhile, it's clutter.
- If you haven't used it in a year, it's clutter.
- If you find yourself defending the object because of how much it cost you, it's clutter.
- If the item makes you feel out of sorts, it's clutter.
- Always remove from your home what you know to be clutter. Otherwise, it will continue to detract from your life.
- No clutter is labeled CLUTTER. Clutter is invisible. It was put in its location subconsciously. That's why you

have to ask if each thing is truly helpful to you or if it's
clutter. Sometimes the most cherished thing is clutter.
Count on it. If it's not useful to you *now*, toss it.

- People can be clutter. Be honest in your relationships. If
  knowing someone diminishes you, she is clutter. You
  can speak honestly with her and see if she can change.
  If not, you can just let her go.

- Toss or give away gifts that you don't like.

- Most photos are clutter. You were trying to preserve a
  moment that felt good to you in that moment. But now
  it's over. You are collecting ghosts. Ghosts are dull
  impressions of the original event. Do you want to live
  among ghosts, or do you want to live in the vibrant living world? Only keep the photos that resonate with this
  moment.

- Feel good about the process of tossing, and avoid the
  guilt. Advertisers taught you that things are more valuable than you. They were wrong. You are right.

- Keep the things that feel alive to you. Things have
  either a living or a dead essence. When you clutter bust
  your life and home, you will very quickly become aware
  of the difference, and you will drop the dead things into
  the trash can.

- Be ruthless. Clutter will try to trick you. Question
  everything.

- First impressions are always correct. If your first feeling is that the thing is clutter, it is. No dumpster diving.

- Your activities can be clutter. I guarantee that something that you are doing in your life now is clutter. You

may be thinking that your value is determined by the activities in your life. That is untrue. You are already valuable! There is no need to prove anything. Those days are over. Ask, "What makes me happy?" Whatever is left over, toss.

- Any piece of clutter could be the thing that stands between you and your happiness. Nothing is too small to be disregarded. Every piece of clutter keeps you from rolling down the freeway of your life with the windows open and your favorite songs playing, with you singing along.

- Toss the trophies, the things that you own only because they are "valuable." Anything you own to impress others is a waste of your time. No one cares.

- Toss anything that makes you feel that the past is more special than right now, that gives you the feeling that life will never be as good as it once was. I don't care how old you are or what you're doing in your life — you are sitting on a gold mine: *you*, and the current state of your heart and life. *The past is as insignificant as old dishwater.* Only keep what reflects your life as significant in this moment.

- Nothing should be under your bed.

- You may come across an item that you know is clutter but that you find difficult to toss. Just remember that in a short while you will either forget all about it or not be able to believe how hard you hung on to the thing.

- Make your bedroom a peaceful sanctuary. Toss anything that agitates or distracts you.

- Have only one TV in the house. Watching a lot of TV is lifestyle clutter. Have the most limited cable package. You can watch only one channel at a time.

- Limit your CDs or MP3 albums to fewer than a hundred. Keep only the music that you will actually listen to now.

- Toss anything that is broken, that can't be fixed, or that you won't take to be fixed.

- Watch your thoughts and become aware of the mental clutter. Your awareness will naturally sift out this clutter.

- Be kind to yourself in the process of tossing. Go at your own pace. Drink plenty of water throughout, and make sure to have snacks by your side.

- Take breaks in clutter busting if you are getting overwhelmed. Take a walk outside.

- You can't organize until you toss the clutter.

- Put nothing in storage. Storage is clutter alimony and a waste of your money.

- Avoid the habit of hiding things that you don't want to look at. Even if something is buried at the bottom of a box, underneath other clutter, it still affects you. Everything you own is attached to you in a subtle way. It will drag you down.

- Toss things that you think lend you an image. You are fooling yourself. You are not a style. You alone are more than enough.

- Walk through your house. When you find your attention sinking like an anchor in a particular spot, stop. Your clutter radar has gone off. Investigate judiciously.

- Only your feelings matter. Avoid asking someone if you should keep something. Trust whatever you decide.

- If you suddenly think of something as clutter, it is. Toss it — now.

- Either give your clutter to charity, post it on an online Freecycle site, or put it out on the curb for someone else to find. Having a garage sale spells procrastination for most people, and whatever doesn't sell usually ends up back in the house. Be strong. Let it go. You are intuitive. Trust your decisions.

- Be patient. There's no need to push yourself or try to clutter bust your entire place in one sitting. Approach one area at a time.

- Clutter is sticky. Look for things that have piled up or been layered together. Chances are you can toss it all.

- If you are in a good relationship or want to be, toss old relationship reminders: love letters and emails and special gifts from old lovers. These keep you trapped in ghostly memories of the heart.

- Trying to keep memories alive in *things* is like trapping a ghost in a box. It will always be a ghost.

- Have fun!

ACKNOWLEDGMENTS

I'm thankful for the inspiration and encouragement I got from my friends Andrew Rymer, Dr. Ron Holman, Lisa Cole, Mark Monroe, Gregory Gardner, Craig Shaynak, Diane Senffner, Kati Duncan, and Wayne Liquorman.

I'd like to thank the wonderful people at New World Library for publishing my book, specifically my editor, Georgia Hughes; my copyeditor, Mimi Kusch; and my publicists, Monique Muhlenkamp and Munro Magruder. Thanks also go to Kristen Cashman for keeping this book on schedule, to Mary Ann Casler for the great cover, to Tona Pearce Myers for typesetting, and to Jonathan Wichmann for editorial assistance.

And a special thank-you to Julia Mossbridge for coming into my life and shining a light in my heart.

I'd also like to thank my clients, whose personal discoveries while clutter busting allowed me to bring my message to you.

I'm grateful that you have decided to allow great and mighty positive change into your life. Your life will thank you in return.

ABOUT THE AUTHOR

Brooks Palmer has been helping clients clear clutter from their homes, garages, offices, and lives for nearly a decade. He also performs stand-up comedy regularly in Chicago, Los Angeles, and New York. He is a member of the Screen Actors' Guild and has appeared in several commercials and films. Palmer divides his time between Chicago and Los Angeles. Visit his clutter-busting website and blog at www.ClutterBusting.com and his humor and creativity website at www.BetterLateThanDead.com.